HIDDEN DANGERS OF THE INTERNET

Brother Wes —

Blessings!

to you!

[signature]

Hidden Dangers of the Internet

Using It without Abusing It

Gregory L. Jantz, Ph.D

with Ann McMurray

Harold Shaw Publishers
Wheaton, Illinois

All Scripture quotations, unless otherwise indicated, are taken from the HOLY BIBLE, NEW INTERNATIONAL VERSION®. NIV®. Copyright © 1973, 1978, 1984 International Bible Society. Used by permission of Zondervan Publishing House. All rights reserved.

The "NIV" and "New International Version" trademarks are registered in the United States Patent and Trademark Office by International Bible Society. Use of either trademark requires permission of International Bible Society.

Scripture quotations marked NLT are taken from the *Holy Bible,* New Living Translation, copyright © 1996. Used by permission of Tyndale House Publishers, Inc., Wheaton, Illinois 60189. All rights reserved.

ISBN 0-87788-149-9

Cover design by David LaPlaca

Library of Congress Cataloging-in-Publication Data

Jantz, Gregory L.
  Hidden dangers of the Internet / by Gregory Jantz, with Ann McMurray
      p.   cm.
    ISBN 0-87788-149-9
      1. Internet addicts—Religious life.   2. Internet addiction—Religious aspects—Christianity.
  I. McMurray, Ann.   II. Title
  BV4596.I57J36   1998
    303.48'33—dc21   98-27612

---

03 02 01 00 99 98
10 9 8 7 6 5 4 3 2 1

TABLE OF CONTENTS

ACKNOWLEDGMENTS

This book was a major challenge. Technology is changing nearly every hour. Our goal is to provide solid, balanced answers to this complex issue.

I am grateful to have had the joy of working with Ann McMurray. Her writing skill and heartbeat for Internet issues were essential.

Our editor, Joan Guest, as always saw the vision and need for this work. To have such an editor is a blessing.

INTRODUCTION

According to a recent Commerce Department report, traffic on the Internet doubles every one hundred days. That means the Internet is growing faster than all other previous technologies. It took radio thirty-eight years to claim fifty million listeners. Television took only thirteen years to claim the same number of viewers. Yet the Internet had over fifty million users in a mere four years. Worldwide users now number over a hundred million. Internet use is exploding. Many people are daily discovering the benefits of this new medium. Its potential for aiding mankind is beyond measure.

The Internet used to be the domain solely of government agencies and computer experts. Now, people from all walks of life are going online from the comfort of their own homes, schools, and offices. Gone is the stereotypical image of a computer nerd, eyes glued to a monitor, oblivious to anything and everything else around him. Replacing him is a picture of just about anybody: male and female, single and married, worker and student, young and old, wealthy and barely making it.

The rapid growth of the Internet has largely outpaced our ability to understand what the effects of this dynamic medium are on our society in general and on people individually. But research is catching up. As more and more people integrate Internet use into their personal and business lives, patterns are beginning to emerge. Businesses all over the world are taking advantage of the economic opportunities. Law enforcement agencies have begun to respond to the illegal activity carried out on this vast, unregulated landscape. The mental health community is investigating the psychological effects of Internet use. As more and more people devote more and more time to the Internet, the question is arising: Are there negative consequences of spending time online? Certainly, all of the answers aren't in, but the ones that are, are sometimes disturbing.

In my position as founder and executive director of the Center for Counseling and Health Resources, Inc., in Edmonds, Washington, I have witnessed firsthand the compelling power of the Internet. I use the Internet in the course of my business and personal life, and I use it to reach out to hurting people through the Center's Web page (www.aplaceofhope.com). However, more individuals and family members are coming to the Center for help in controlling their Internet use. For them, the Internet is not some benign high-tech tool. I have counseled individuals whose personal and work relationships are in a shambles due to the amount of time they spend online each day. I have met with families ripped apart when one member's use of the Internet takes priority over all other established relationships.

It doesn't have to be that way. Internet users do not have to be caught in its web. I have developed a whole-person approach that takes into consideration each person's emotional, relational, physical, nutritional, and spiritual components. In this book, I weigh the facts and offer biblical, common-sense solutions to this high-tech problem, helping individuals recover the balance they desire in their lives.

This is not a book about the benefits of the Internet or the practical aspects of using it. Those topics are covered well in other books and magazines. In this book I focus on the problems that sometimes arise and how we can prevent or fix them. The suggestions for help include general items and those especially aimed at the Christian reader. Anyone struggling with this issue will profit from taking a whole-person approach to it, including confronting it with the weapons of the Spirit.

CHAPTER ONE

LIFE IN THE FAST LANE:

How Technology Has Changed Experience

Bzzzzzzz! Your alarm goes off annoyingly.

You're late! In a rush, you propel yourself out of bed. Good thing you set the automatic brew function on your coffee machine last night. No time to waste this morning!

You hit the shower, blurry-eyed but determined to get wet—and dry—in record time. No time to read the paper or watch the morning news shows, so you turn on the waterproof radio suction-cupped to the shower tile.

Grabbing your tankard of coffee and a prepackaged breakfast bar, you're out the door. You gun the car out of the drive and shoot down the highway. With a sense of relief, you roar your car up the on-ramp and revel in uninterrupted speed. You weave in and out of traffic, maintaining your momentum.

At work, you screech into a parking space. Entering the office, you try to appear as if you're really not running. Fill up your coffee. Dash into your office. Ready for the morning! Your day is propelled by a sense of fragile momentum, ever-threatening to devolve into chaos. Pandemonium kept at arm's length.

As the shadows lengthen into afternoon, the sense of being behind looms ever larger. Before you know it, the afternoon is gone and you're stuck in evening traffic on the freeway. The

> Instantaneous communications are helping to prove it really is a small world after all.

sheer waste of your time is unfathomable. You may not be going anywhere in your car, but your mind is racing. What do you have to do tomorrow? The day after? Next week? You call your voice mail at work and leave a message to remember something vital tomorrow.

When you get home, dinner is two minutes on high in the microwave; it takes about as long to eat as it did to heat up. You settle into your chair, pick up the remote, turn on the television and simultaneously watch three shows. Every commercial is an invitation to change channels and check out what you're missing.

Welcome to Life in the Fast Lane, where every second counts.

Everything You Could Wish For

Within a short span of years, technology has hard-wired itself into an increasing portion of everyday life. From the coffee maker to the cell phone to the computer, devices have promised to free our lives of wait. *Waiting* is now synonymous with *wasting*. If time is money, waiting is wasteful.

And if waiting is wasteful, you become wasteful if you are not utilizing each moment to its full potential. You've now got to squeeze as much productivity out of your schedule and out of your life as you can possibly tolerate.

Everything You Wanted to Know
Instantaneous communications are helping to prove it really is

a small world after all. Your community isn't just the city you live in; your community is global. Turn on the television and CNN could just as easily be showing a live feed from Pakistan as from Philadelphia. Events and situations that used to be far away and, somehow, removed can now be broadcast live into your home; now triumphs and tragedies thousands of miles away can carry as much impact as if they'd happened just down the street. Distance, both physical and emotional, is harder to maintain.

Now, add the Internet into the mix, with its endless avenues of information. So many choices, so many paths to explore. From the need for speed in our fast-paced society to the need for information in our ever-expanding global neighborhood to the need for human connection in an increasingly isolated world, the Internet promises to be everything you could wish for.

With constant updates from Internet news agencies, there is no need to even wait until eleven to catch the evening news. In fact, for some, Internet news sites and online newspapers and magazines have replaced printed sources of information. There is no excuse not to know about—and experience—the latest disaster, no matter how far away it is.

Computers and the Internet have provided us with what we've apparently always wanted—an ongoing, constant stream of information, without ever having to leave home. The slogan of the day has gone from "Don't leave home without it" to simply, "Don't leave home." Need to know about Belize for a report at school? You used to have to trudge down to your neighborhood library and pore through stacks of reference books. Not anymore. Online encyclopedias and Web sites can provide instant information. Need to know who makes a certain type of fiberglass insulation for a business client? You used to have to pick your brain, pick someone else's brain, get out the phone book, and spend hours on the phone tracking down sources. Now, you just log onto the Internet, type *fiberglass* into a search engine, and pick through your choice of sites to visit, all with information freely available.

Whatever You Want, Whenever You Want It

Technology can be a real time-saver. Over the Internet, time zones have no meaning. It may be four o'clock in the morning and everyone around you is asleep, but it's early afternoon in the United Kingdom. Someone there is up. Need a fast answer or a quick response? No problem! Somewhere, someone is always awake.

Nobody at home to talk to? Nobody there who really understands? Need someone to tell your troubles to? Just dive into the Internet. There's a vast pool of people waiting to lend a listening ear. You can't just lean over the backyard fence anymore and talk to your neighbor; the fence is six-feet high and they've got a really mean dog. Instead, hop online to your favorite chat room and someone there will not only listen to you, they'll empathize with everything you say. Companionship and compassion are just a few keystrokes away.

Be Careful What You Wish For

What's the problem? Wasn't all this technology created to make everyday life better? Isn't this what we've always dreamed of? (Or, at least, what Bill Gates has always dreamed of?) Are we never satisfied? Technology was supposed to make things so much better—and, in very many ways, it has. So why doesn't it always feel better? If the Internet is such a universal blessing, why have some people come to view it as a curse?

Reacting vs. Responding

Could it be that waiting isn't always wasteful? In fact, there are times when waiting can be useful, even necessary. Our minds work faster than computers, at least for now. We absorb information at a rate even the quickest computer CPU would envy. But thinking and decision making are not just about absorbing; they also involve processing. Analysis takes time. It's not just a matter of compiling data. It involves merging information with experience and application. Reacting is immediate. Responding takes time.

In your blind rush to speed forward, do you really have the time you need to figure out where you're going? Focused pursuit of a goal is admirable. However, an uncontrolled rush for the sake of forward motion proves you're moving, but it doesn't guarantee you'll end up anywhere worthwhile. And when you do stop, only to find it is not really where you wanted to be, how much time have you wasted during all that rushing around? Sometimes, slowing down actually *saves* time.

In the Bible's account of Creation, we're told that on the seventh day, God the Creator rested. If God, in his omnipotence, could take a day off, why do we think we have to be busy all of the time to be useful? And not only did God set up some regular time off for us on a weekly basis, known as the Sabbath, but he also created us with the physical necessity to take time off on a daily basis. It's called sleep—you know, that stuff you never seem to get enough of.

Whether on a daily or weekly basis, human beings simply need some down time. Time to take a breather from our hectic schedules, to rest, relax, and process the flotsam and jetsam of our lives. It's not wasting; it's refreshing.

Won't You Be My Neighbor?

A global community sounds wonderful. A whole world without artificial barriers. A world connected by human thought and action instead of one separated by physical boundaries. A global community where everyone is your neighbor. But how many neighbors can you actually keep track of? How many places, how many people, can you care about before your compassion thins? And what does it mean to have a "neighbor" thousands of miles away, connected by the Internet, while you ignore the neighbor next door? How far does being your brother's keeper extend?

Garbage in, Garbage Out

Sure, there's a gazillion gigabytes of information available on the Internet, but how do you know how accurate it is? Much of that information is presented without a source beyond the address it was obtained from. Information from Site A is passed on and slightly modified in Site B. Site C opens Site B and spreads that information, altering it again, but never referencing Site A. The more controversial, the more extraordinary the information, the more the tendency to comment, to embellish, to expound—all of which gets passed on. It's like that old game of telephone, where you line up a number of people and pass on a piece of information from ear to ear to ear. The information recited by the last person rarely resembles what was spoken by the first person in line. With millions of people using the Internet, that line can get very long.

> What happens if this neutral technology becomes an increasingly negative influence in our lives?

On Call

If you have the ability over the Internet to make contact with anybody at anytime, remember, so do they. The Internet is not just a place for you to get your needs met by other people. It's also a place for other people to contact you to meet their needs. The more people you contact, the more people will come knocking at your e-mail box. The day may come, or may have already arrived, when you've hopped online to fill your own needs and found yourself spending all of your time dealing with the demands and desires of others. Companionship is just fine, but sometimes the price is a nearly endless list of e-mail messages.

Caught in a Causal Loop

The computer, and the Internet it gives us access to, has changed the way we live and interact. It has done so in response to changes in how we already live and interact. You might say the computer and this society we live in exist in a causal loop: cause-effect-cause-effect-cause, etc. The computer, designed to meet a certain set of needs, ends up fueling a need we didn't realize we had. It then responds in a way we didn't anticipate. Is it any wonder the world of technology reinvents itself continuously?

One might say we've become co-dependent with the computer and the Internet. They enable us to go where we want without condemnation or comment. There will be no intervention, no "family meeting" where the computer is concerned. In fact, it's *not* concerned—about us or about what we do on it. It is just a machine. How we use it is totally up to us.

So what happens when we're unwilling or unable to regulate our own actions regarding the computer and the Internet? What happens if this neutral technology becomes an increasingly negative influence in our lives? Because this technology is so new, so fast, so fluctuating, there is very little information about its negative side for most users (a word that previously referred to drug addicts—a coincidence?).

The media has certainly advertised the negative aspects of the Internet. Stories abound about predators who stalk the Internet, searching to exploit, molest, and abuse the naive. While this type of "news" is readily available, the more subtle problems relating to the Internet are not so easy to come by. Some of this has to do with the fact that the Internet is still relatively new; there hasn't been enough time to judge and evaluate long-term use. A small contingent of people (primarily university researchers and scientists) have been surfing the Net for twenty years or more, but most people have discovered this technological phenomenon quite recently. Habitual, destructive patterns are still emerging.

Internet Addiction Survey

One of those who has begun to study the effects of prolonged Internet use is Dr. Kimberly Young, a professor at the University of Pittsburgh at Bradford. At the 105th meeting of the American Psychological Association in Chicago, Illinois, in August of 1997, Dr. Young presented the findings of a survey she developed entitled "Internet Addiction Survey." The respondents to her detailed questionnaire available online were young and middle-aged, male and female, professional and blue-collar. Those who appeared to be most susceptible to uncontrolled online use were individuals who had a lot of time on their hands—people who stayed at home, were unemployed, underemployed, or college students.

Respondents were classified as dependent Internet users if they met four or more of the following criteria over the period of a year:

- Feel preoccupied with the Internet (thinking about it while offline)
- Feel a need to spend increasing amounts of time on the Internet in order to achieve satisfaction
- Have an inability to control their Internet use
- Feel restless or irritable when attempting to cut down or stop Internet use
- Use the Internet as a way of escaping from problems or of relieving a poor mood (feelings of helplessness, guilt, anxiety, or depression)

- Lie to family members or friends to conceal the extent of involvement with the Internet
- Jeopardize or risk the loss of a significant relationship, job, or educational or career opportunity because of the Internet
- Keep returning even after spending an excessive amount of money on online fees
- Go through withdrawal when offline (increased depression, anxiety)
- Stay online longer than originally intended

If you've picked up this book, it's because you've been asking your own questions about the Internet. Take a moment and review the list above, for yourself or for someone you're concerned about. Remember, if you fit four or more of them, it indicates the Internet is being misused. You owe it to yourself or to the person you're concerned about to do more than just admit there is a problem.

In successive chapters, you will read about common user pitfalls as they are currently defined. You'll also be given practical and biblical solutions to overcoming Internet abuse. Remember, while technology changes at a mind-numbing rate, human nature changes very little and God changes not at all. The Internet may be new, but people and their reactions aren't.

One Problem—Two Sections

This book has been divided into two sections. Section One is written to the person who is worried about a loved one's use or misuse of the Internet. Section Two is written to the online user who has concerns either about the amount of time being spent online or the types of activities he or she is participating in online.

At the end of each chapter in Section One, there are "How to Respond" suggestions. An appropriate response by you to a friend or loved one can go a long way toward helping that person decide if there is a problem with their Internet use. At the end of each chapter in Section Two, there are "How to Change" suggestions. One of the most effective ways to change behavior is to substitute appropriate, healthy behavior for destructive, unhealthy habits. Some chapters also include assignments to get you thinking about key points in the chapter and how to apply them to your own situation, and most chapters include relevant biblical material for the Christian reader.

While it might be tempting to read only the section you feel applies to you, you will benefit from reading both. Most readers will probably know people who fall into the "other" category. It is important to be able to view the Internet through their eyes. Take the time to do that, and you'll be blessed with deeper understanding of them and of yourself.

SECTION ONE

FOR CONCERNED FAMILY MEMBERS AND FRIENDS

CHAPTER TWO

Internet 101

Figuring Out the Terms and the Geography

It seems as though wherever you turn now, everyone is buzzing about the Internet. The Internet is likely to be leaving its mark on more and more of your familiar surroundings. Look at the bottom of most magazine ads and there is a string of letters and symbols, usually beginning with "www." It's like a secret handshake, and maybe you aren't yet a member of the club. Half of the holiday updates from people you know include an e-mail address. Some people seem more proud of being online than they were of a job promotion or an addition to the family!

Computer Confusion

If you are not yet an Internet user, you may be wondering what it's all about. And if you have a family member or friend who has gone "whole hog" into the online world, you may be wondering if you should be worried.

The Internet need not be a confusing mass of destinations with an incomprehensible vocabulary. It's really just an immense meeting place—a combination global bazaar, communication exchange, electronic coffee shop, message center, and play land. The global bazaar is called the *World Wide Web*. The communication exchange is *Usenet*. *Chat rooms* are the electronic coffee shops. The message center is the phenomenon known as *e-mail*. And what kid doesn't like to play in *MUD*—*multiuser domains* (electronic role-playing "environments")? Each area has a specific function and attracts different kinds of people.

> The Internet: global bazaar, communication exchange, electronic coffee shop, message center, play land.

Not every area presents a problem to an Internet user. What hooks one person may be no problem to another. The degree of intense participation and the resulting danger for abuse differ depending upon which part is entered. A brief explanation of each area of the Internet will help identify potential problem areas. As you seek to determine how to help someone control use of the Internet, you'll need to be aware of which parts of the Internet are being used.

At Home on the Web

The area of the Internet most people have heard about is the World Wide Web. The World Wide Web is an ever-expanding collection of Web pages or *home pages* comprised of information designed and maintained by individuals, organizations, educational institutions, and businesses.

Individuals make home pages to let others know who they are, their history, their likes and dislikes. Home pages can include text, graphics, and/or music and video clips. Text from a wedding ceremony, pictures of a new baby, video from a dance recital or the latest vacation, new address and phone information, genealogical information—all can be posted on a home page. They are as individual as, well, individuals. Each is a way of saying, "This is who I am and what I like. Come, take a look." These individual home pages can also include links to other Web sites that the page creator finds of special interest, for example, the official site of a favorite TV series or an online bookstore. They often include a place for visitors to leave a message. Some home pages will include a numerical counter so the creator and visitors can know how many *hits,* or visits to the site, there have been.

Organizations and educational institutions maintain Web sites to provide the public with information as to who they are and what their aims or goals are. As more and more people utilize Web pages as a primary source of information regarding these organizations and institutions, the amount and type of information grows to keep pace with demand.

This leads directly into why businesses maintain Web pages: consumer demand. Consumers = Customers = Profit. For businesses, Web pages are another form of advertising, another way to get their message to a segment of consumers. From mega-corporations like Nike and Coca-Cola to local businesses, it seems any business that wants to stay ahead of the competition—or just keep up—has a Web address.

Likewise, churches and other ministries have found in the Internet a vast, ripe field for harvesting. Web surfers with spiritual questions, casual browsers, and those in deep spiritual pain all go to the Internet for help and information.

Many businesses and ministries now use Web pages as a source of first contact. This advertising is both informational and interactive. In other words, if a business sends a flyer to you in the mail, it's one-way, scattershot. You didn't ask for the flyer. They sent it to you whether you wanted it or not. Because of that, the percentage of responses to advertising of that nature is very small. But when you visit a business Web site, you are making a conscious decision to contact the busi-

> ## The Internet is designed to capture attention, and it works.

ness. So the more informational, the more interesting, the more catchy the Web site is, the better.

Is it any wonder people like to surf the Net, looking at all these different Web sites? It's a veritable cornucopia of fascinating stuff, specifically designed to draw people in with bright colors, attractive fonts, and eye-catching graphics. It's designed to capture attention, and it works.

When a person first gains access to the Web, the thousands upon thousands of sites to explore can be overwhelming. In fact, the only way to make sense of it all is through using some of the *search engines* available. A search engine acts as a guide to the Internet user, helping locate sites containing specific words or bits of information that are of interest. And because of the sheer number of sites available under even a moderately specific search, it can take hours and hours to sift through all of the available information. It's kind of like eating sunflower seeds; you have to crack open a lot of shells to get a relatively small amount of meat.

While it might seem that this kind of activity has the potential to snare Internet users, preliminary research does not bear this out. According to information gathered in Dr. Young's Internet addiction survey, this type of Net surfing accounts for, at most, 9 percent of those respondents who fit the pattern of Internet dependence. According to Dr. Young, database searches—while interesting and often time-consuming—are not the actual reasons dependents become addicted to the Internet. (It needs to be noted that Dr. Young's study included only 496 participants, and study in this area is relatively new. But it seems to suggest that the percentage of those who abuse the Internet because of Net surfing is small.) Of course, if the person you're concerned about is part of this small percentage, he or she is just as trapped in that behavior, or, rather, in the inability to moderate that behavior, as any other.

If the person you are concerned about is new to the Net and seems to have gone over the deep end in a pursuit of interesting Web sites, understand that this is pretty normal. What seems to happen is a cyber version of the old movie *The Lost Weekend.* Newcomers discover this medium and can't really believe it. They end up spending their evening hours or their first few weekends jumping in with both feet, not particularly caring where they land. Wherever they land, whatever topic tickles their fancy at the moment, they're sure to find something of interest. So in they plunge, not unlike someone who can't put down a John Grisham novel or the latest edition of *The Sporting News.*

This initial period is intense, no doubt; but for most users it's also over quickly. Before long, either they have decided they have seen all they want to on a subject (how many hang gliding sites do you really want to gain access to?) or they get overloaded—and bored. The Web is one-way. What seems to hook people in much harder is the interactive, two-way nature of other parts of the Internet.

Good-bye, Snail Mail

E-mail, short for *electronic mail,* is one of the two-way areas of the Internet. It is a way to send messages to other people without having to wait for hand delivery. In fact, people who have discovered the joys of e-mail can grow increasingly frustrated with "snail mail," otherwise known as the regular postal service.

E-mail can be compelling for several reasons. Communication can happen very quickly. In addition, deep levels of communication with another person can be achieved in relatively short order. Finally, very personal e-mail communications can occur between people who are in every other way removed from one another—in essence, strangers apart from what they choose to share online.

It used to be that when you wrote someone a letter, you knew it would take a few days to get there, a few days for the recipient to write a reply, and a few days for the return letter to get back to you. No one expected a speedy response. If it took a couple of weeks to get an answer, well, that was okay. But e-mail's very speed produces an expectation of immediacy.

Immediacy can become confused with urgency. For people who become dependent on their e-mail activity, the messages they send and the replies they wait for aren't just interesting, they're vital. When you write a letter, you accept the time lag involved. You get on with your life while you wait for a response. Not so with e-mail. If a message is sent while the other person is online, their *Internet service provider* (ISP) will inform that person of the incoming message, and it can be read and responded to immediately.

Even the most mundane of communications can take on an unrealistic sense of importance because of the speed with which it can be handled. After all, in other areas of life, if something's really important, it earns a quick response. Conversely, if something is responded to quickly, it must be important. And important messages can transfer importance to the one sending or receiving the message. For some people, this sense of being important, of being relevant, can be a tremendous draw if their other daily interactions fail to produce the same sort of satisfaction. Through e-mail, people can get noticed.

> **Through e-mail, people can get noticed.**

Often, those e-mailing back and forth are acquainted with each other. Face to face, they have traded addresses and begun an electronic relationship. This relationship has the capacity to evolve over time, given the nature of the Internet. Within relationships, surface discussions gradually move into deeper and more intimate territory as the relationship and trust grow. With e-mail, this progression can be fast-forwarded, spurred on by the speed and remote nature of e-mail messages. Unlike actually talking back and forth, e-mailers only see their words scrolling across a computer monitor. Questions they might never have the courage to ask, let alone answer, in person take on a different feel when reduced to on-screen text. There is no one to see a red-faced, sheepish response to a personal query.

Of course, e-mailers also communicate with people they have never actually met. Addresses may be obtained from a variety of sources, allowing for virtual strangers to begin online relationships. It is within this veil of anonymity that problems can occur. Anonymity, producing a false sense of security, can remove a natural inhibition for caution, especially when discussing items of a personal or intimate nature. In fact, it is not unheard of for online relationships to develop a strength powerful enough to draw people out of established, real life relationships and into a physical relationship with someone met over the Internet.

Panning for Internet Gold

Another two-way arena of the Internet is called *Usenet,* the general term given to the Internet's thousands of newsgroups. *Newsgroup* doesn't necessarily mean "news" as it is traditionally defined. Newsgroups are computer bulletin boards on virtually any subject. You post a message on the bulletin board and you can read and respond to the messages others have left. Scanning a newsgroup can be like pan-

> Scanning a newsgroup can be like panning for gold.

ning for gold: for some people, the chance to yell "Eureka!" is worth the hours spent picking through a bunch of useless chunks in order to find that golden nugget of information.

Finding an identity, a purpose in life, through a shared interest is not uncommon. It is one of the reasons religious and civic organizations abound. In the past distance created a hurdle for people wanting to gather around a common interest. There might simply not be enough people interested in any given community to warrant forming a group. The Internet, however, draws from a global community. The number of people from which to form a group is now considerably larger. And the number of interests to attract people is also vast. No longer does someone have to feel alienated or isolated because their interest lies outside the mainstream.

Newsgroups can be formed around any topic—from current events to areas devoted to popular television shows. Every time your loved one starts to expound on Topic A, your eyes may glaze over. After a solid hour of nothing else but Topic A, you may be ready to say, "Get a life!" But because of the Topic A newsgroup on the Internet, your loved one will find a host of people who are just as convinced that Topic A *is* life. Therein lies the difficulty and the tremendous draw these newsgroups have: They tend to draw in people who truly do live to discuss certain topics.

Meeting for Chat

Just like newsgroups, *chat rooms* provide two-way communication but with the added bonus of immediate response. With a newsgroup, or bulletin board, you need to wait until your message is noticed and responded to. When you join in a chat room, you get to "talk" with whomever else is online at the same time you are. The communication is immediate. True, chat room communication is still done by typing messages, but those messages travel back and forth virtually instantaneously between occupants of the chat room. Your fingers do the talking.

Many ISPs have chat rooms for their subscribers. Any person who uses that ISP can gain access to the chat room. In addition, private chat rooms can be set up, with the person who sets up the room having control over which other subscribers have access to it.

Chat rooms provide a sense of intimacy and togetherness even more compelling than e-mail. People who frequent the same rooms soon develop a relationship with each other. They get used to who will be online and when. Often, people will agree when to meet next, or they have a set time to be online together.

In addition to immediacy and intimacy, chat rooms also provide anonymity. In a chat room, no one needs to know who you really are. You communicate through an online personality (sometimes called an *avatar*), the high-tech equivalent of a CB radio "handle." Being anonymous provides some people with the freedom they feel they need to be totally honest. Or totally dishonest.

Just like e-mail, the conversations carried on through chat rooms can become intense and intimate very quickly. The more frequent and involved the relationship, the more intense it becomes. The more intense it becomes, the more compelling the reasons to continue. These reasons can overtake reason itself and leave a person spending inappropriate amounts of time communicating inappropriate types of information. This is the type of behavior you will need to watch out for if the person you're concerned about is becoming Internet dependent.

As you observe or discuss these activities with your loved one, be aware that long-term users have developed a kind of shorthand for use in chat rooms (as well as e-mail and newsgroup correspondence). The facial cues that would be present in face-to-face meetings are replaced by punctuation that viewed sideways resembles such things as smiles or winking faces—for example, :-) and ;-). These are called *emoticons*. Internet shorthand also includes shortened combinations of letters to represent words or phrases, such as "lol" for "laugh out loud" and "rotfl" for "rolling on the floor laughing." There are entire Web pages devoted to providing glossaries of such expressions and emoticons.

Play Time

Online gaming is another area of the Internet that exerts a strong draw. Games on the Internet are known as *MUDs,* multiuser domains (or "dungeons"). They began as essentially text-only, online versions of role-playing games like Dungeons and Dragons. Castles, wizards, villains, dragons, and demons are all part of a MUD landscape. In addition, MUDs generally have a game master who monitors the game, defines its rules, helps newcomers, and mediates disputes between players. Many of these games are still available on the Internet in a text-only format.

> Games are exciting, physically and intellectually demanding, and intensely interactive.

Recently, however, MUDs have included a graphics component, not unlike a video game played through a Nintendo or Sony system. Medieval-style games have been joined by other popular genres, such as science-fiction space adventures. In addition, through a private chat room set up exclusively for players of a MUD, Internet gamers can now not only pit their skills against other actual players, but they can also conduct a running conversation with whomever else is playing the game at the same time.

The dual combination of playing a real person, as opposed to a computer-generated opponent, coupled with the ability to actually converse with other players of the game makes online gaming a potent draw for some Internet users. These games are exciting, physically and intellectually demanding, and intensely interactive. The visual images and immediate communication can easily engulf an online gamer in an entirely different world.

How to Respond

If you suspect or are convinced that a problem exists with someone you care about regarding their Internet use, you will need to prepare yourself to communicate your concern.

Examine Your Heart

Ask yourself what is motivating your concern. Are you worried more about how much time is being spent online or how little time is being spent with you? Make sure your approach is centered on your concern for your loved one, not a backhanded attempt to get something you want for yourself.

When you convey your concern to your family member or friend, you are going to be making a value judgment based on how that person is using his or her time. Before you can do this, however, you will need to evaluate how you are using your time. To use an analogy from the Bible, it may be necessary for you to remove the log from your own eye before you attempt to remove the splinter from someone else's. In other words, if you are spending multiple hours a day talking on the telephone, reading a suspense or romance novel, or watching television, the force of your concern over Internet use may be significantly diluted.

Be Aware

Find out which areas of the Internet seem to pose the greatest problem for the person you're concerned about. Make a record of the types of activities being engaged in and the amount of time being spent online in each activity. This doesn't mean standing over the computer with a notebook and pencil in your hands and a dour expression on your face. What it does mean is being alert and aware. As you have opportunity to interact, ask questions and become informed.

Don't be surprised if your inquiries are initially rebuffed. If you have shown no interest in the Internet before or if your interest has always been expressed in the negative, you may need to persevere by showing an open and inquisitive nature, without being judgmental. Be prepared to change your mind. You may be coming at this problem with preconceived notions and opinions. Some of those could very well be in error. Take the time necessary to be sure of yourself before you confront the person you're concerned about.

Pray for Spiritual Guidance

Whenever I face a situation that has the potential to turn into a confrontation, I make sure that prayer precedes that contact. Prayer provides calm and clarity.

If the person you are concerned about has become dependent on the Internet, your attempt to alert her or him to that dependence may not be initially appreciated. That person may very well react angrily to your snooping or meddling into a private matter. Trading shouts is not the most effective way to communicate your concern. Remaining calmly in control in the face of a potential outburst can help to diffuse the emotions of the situation, allowing reason to come to the forefront.

Often, when confronted with a dependence on a certain behavior or activity, the person affected will offer a variety of excuses as to why that behavior or activity is really not harmful. These excuses are defense mechanisms to allow continuing the activity, even when confronted with the harm being done. To counter these excuses, you will need the clarity provided by prayer to see through the smoke screen into the truth of the situation.

No matter how much opposition you encounter as you attempt to convey your concern, remember, you have a powerful ally in your corner. God is even more concerned than you are. It is God's desire for all people to avoid activities that entangle them in destructive behavior.

The Next Step

1. Write down the areas of the Internet where you suspect the person you care about is having trouble.

2. If you told your loved one that he or she would not be able to go online for a day, a week, a month, or ever again, what would be the response? Are you fearful thinking about what the response would be?

3. Spend some time in prayer, asking God to help you make sure your intentions are focused primarily on the good of the other person. As you examine your own heart and life, ask God to help you respond positively to any areas in your own life that need to be changed.

CHAPTER THREE

Are You a Technophobe?

Making Sure Your Loved One's Problem Isn't Yours

Sometimes Charlie just couldn't understand his wife. As far as he was concerned, Carolyn had gone out and spent good money on a bunch of fancy junk. She seemed to think it was the greatest thing in the world; for him, all it meant was thousands of dollars flying out of their bank account. And it wasn't like they had all that much to spare, either. But he wasn't going to cause a big deal over it. After all, she was so excited and happy.

When it came to computers, Charlie felt absolutely lost. When Carolyn took him along on her shopping trips, he just stood in the aisles feeling shocked, baffled by the strange terminology and the salespeople who all seemed to speak a foreign language called computerese.

His company had added a new computer system a couple of years ago. Most of the "kids" in the office tried to teach him how to operate it, but he didn't understand a word they said. He'd finally reverted to a few laughs and "can't teach an old dog new tricks." He retired pretty soon after that.

Then Carolyn brought a computer into their house. It seemed to just grow in the spare bedroom overnight. Before long, there was the printer, then speakers, then shelves to fit all of the books, paper, floppy disks that weren't the least bit floppy, and CDs, not to mention the magazines that started appearing on their doorstep with even more computer stuff advertised on every page. The darned thing was taking over the bedroom, taking over their life. And his wife couldn't be happier.

The whole thing made him cranky.

Technophobes vs. Technophiles

Do you feel as if you woke up on the wrong side of the bed at the dawn of this technological age? You could be a techno-phobe. And if you are, your prob-lem with someone's use of the In-ternet may have less to do with how much that person uses it and more to do with how much you fear or hate it. This problem can be compounded if the person you care about doesn't just use the computer or tolerate it, but actually loves it. You are a technophobe, and the other person is a technophile. You are opposites and bound to clash. You see things from completely opposite points of view.

> Your problem with someone's use of the Internet may have more to do with how much you hate it.

- Technophiles love the onrushing pace of change. The speed of technology and the infinite possibilities of the Internet can't be fast enough. They are enthralled with what can happen next.

  Technophobes don't understand where this brave new world is going. If society is truly on a fast track, they want to find the quickest way off.

- Technophiles embrace the Internet and its uses as a way to connect with the global village. They are able to look into the face of a computer monitor and connect, not only with the machine itself, but also with everyone they meet online. To them, the machine isn't an impediment to human connection, it's an augmentation.

To technophobes, the computer is a sterile piece of machinery. The idea of making a human connection by sitting for hours in front of a newfangled typewriter is ludicrous. The computer affords the technophobe no ability for expression through action, intonation, or personal style.

- Technophiles love the roller-coaster, thrill-a-minute ride of technological change. They love keeping track of all of the latest technological improvements and gazing starry-eyed into the future. Each new electronic acquisition is greeted with as much enthusiasm as a new baby in the family.

To technophobes, change isn't a roller-coaster ride as much as it's like being dragged behind a powerboat without skis. They have a sense of going so fast, they can't begin to see where they are going, let alone where they are. As a result, they are drowning in technological change.

- Technophiles have no trouble turning on the computer, opening a program, and having at it. They're not afraid to explore, make mistakes, and explore some more. They don't count as wasted the time spent just goofing around on the computer or surfing the Net. They're not always concerned with an end product. The process of searching and learning, of exploring, is gratifying enough for them.

Technophobes, if they ever get on the computer, do so

cautiously, fearfully; ready to scatter like sheep at the sight of anything unfamiliar. Technophobes see a disaster of biblical proportions every time they meet an error screen.

- Technophiles are able to interpret what's on the screen through a form of selective viewing. Since they're familiar with computers in general and the Internet in particular, they focus only on what's absolutely necessary. Even though there is a barrage of information, they're dealing with only a specific amount at any one time. They can disregard almost everything else. And since they are informed users, they don't panic.

  Technophobes look at a computer screen or a Web page and see an overwhelming amount of visual stimuli. They don't understand what's going on, so they can't disregard anything. They have little idea how they ended up where they are and aren't exactly sure where that is or how to leave.

If you are a technophobe, you are predisposed to be suspicious of things on the computer, including the Internet. You may not want to have anything to do with it and can't imagine spending much time on it. So any amount of time anyone else spends on it is incomprehensible and suspicious. Before you automatically assume that someone in your life is Internet dependent, be aware of the possibility you may be exhibiting technophobic tendencies.

How to Respond

If you are a technophobe, the surest way to shed your fear of the computer is to demystify it. Objects are demystified when they are understood. The following are some steps to help you understand the computer and the Internet.

Step One: Be Informed

Find someone from whom you can learn about the computer and the Internet. This is probably going to be someone who is comfortable with the computer—a friend or relative, even the person you are concerned about. However, if he or she shows limited interest in explaining the computer to you because of the amount of time it takes away from personal use of the computer, take note. Consider this a red flag.

Sometimes, finding a disassociated third party is best for learning a new skill. Consider taking a class at a local computer store. Many of today's computer stores

> Find someone from whom you can learn about the computer and the Internet.

are also training centers where consumers can learn to operate programs purchased at the store. For those who do not have the resources to pay for extended computer store training (although costs will vary, and this option should not be dismissed out of course), most community colleges offer classes in popular software programs. If scheduling is a problem and money isn't, consider hiring a private tutor to teach you how to use a computer at home.

Consider getting instruction in hardware, learning how the computer actually works. For some people, anxiety evaporates once they open up the dreaded box and get their hands inside.

Step Two: Start Simple

The next step after learning about the computer and the Internet is for you to find a simple activity on the computer that you can play with. Try a computer game. Many have overcome their fear of using the computer by mastering the simple game of solitaire that comes with Microsoft Windows. One advantage of solitaire is that it is a familiar game; you don't need to learn both the computer and the game. Initially, try a game that is played at the pace of the user, not at the pace of the computer. It may also be best to choose a game without musical accompaniment; you may find that the repetitious background music of some games just increases anxiety.

On the Internet, many first-time users enjoy doing a simple word or subject search on the World Wide Web. Searches can be conducted with only a vague idea of the subject matter and are as easy as clicking the highlighted icon on the search page to connect to a Web site. (Be careful, however, not to click on an icon that takes you to a Web site that costs money. You should be informed of this before you incur a cost.)

As you become comfortable playing a game or using a program, remember to progress at your own pace. If you are being taught by a technophile, he or she may have a tendency to want to fast-forward you to Wing Commander IV after a week playing solitaire. It may be necessary for you to explain that you're comfortable at a certain level and have no intention of moving forward yet. That's fine.

Step Three: Read

To further understand the computer and the Internet, get some good, old-fashioned reading material. There are many books and magazines on computing that are specifically tailored to novice computer users. These resources take into account the reader's unfamiliarity with the subject and present their material in an easily understandable manner. Remember, computing isn't magic. It can be understood by finding the right material for your level of expertise.

Step Four: Accept Reality and Adjust

Computers are here to stay in this society. The speed and ease with which they handle routine functions ensure their future. That is reality.

If, after reading this book, you realize the problem isn't so much with the other person as it is with you, you will need to adjust. That doesn't mean you will have to accept the Internet into your own life. Adjusting may mean you'll simply need to choose to do something you find productive and meaningful while your family member or friend is enjoying online time. Choose to do something that is as personally satisfying and enriching to you as being online is to him or her. When you get back together, you'll both come refreshed and renewed.

When Your Fear Is Justified

Just because you've identified with the feelings of being a technophobe doesn't necessarily mean your friend or loved one doesn't have a problem with Internet abuse. But as you learn more about yourself, the computer, and the Internet, you will be better able to gauge how serious the problem is. Additionally, your new knowledge will enable you to speak more specifically about your concerns. Your loved one will be less able to distract you from your concerns by playing to your ignorance of computers and/or the Internet.

While all of this may seem like a lot of trouble to undergo, especially when it concerns an area you're not all that interested in, remember your motivation. Remember your concern for that other person. His or her connection to the Internet may be obscuring the truth. Your informed perspective may be just the thing needed to bring the situation into focus.

The Next Step

1. Can you relate to some of the same frustrations of a

technophobe? List the three feelings that come first into your mind whenever you think of the computer and/or the Internet.

2. Are you in a relationship with someone who is your "techno" opposite? If so, how has that brought conflict into your relationship? List some ways you have successfully dealt with opposite viewpoints in your relationship—whether or not they specifically concern the computer.

3. Think over the activities you engage in by yourself (for example, reading, exercising, talking on the phone, watching a certain television show). How much time do you spend on each activity? Is your loved one left to find something else to do while you are busy?

4. If you are a technophobe, outline a strategy for becoming more comfortable with the computer and the Internet. Include a timetable for attaining this higher level of comfort.

5. Read 1 Corinthians 9:19-22. Reflect on Paul's concept of becoming all things to all people. How does that concept affect you in regard to the Internet?

CHAPTER FOUR

Taking Parental Control:

If a Child's Computer Use Goes Out of Bounds

It all started out innocently enough, Helen thought. For a while, television was the perfect electronic baby sitter. Jeremy would sit mesmerized, laughing and singing with his TV friends. But his fondness for "Mr. Rogers' Neighborhood" disappeared after he turned four. Jeremy craved the fast-paced action of "Sesame Street." He was so intent on the flashing images, Helen soon realized she could get a lot of chores done while Jeremy was content in front of the television.

As Jeremy got a little older, Helen took on a night job to help with the bills. Because her time at home was increasingly harried, more and more she found herself plopping Jeremy in front of the television—just for an hour or so.

By the time Jeremy was seven, he'd advanced from watching television to *working* television, through the controller of the Nintendo game system Helen and Ed had given him for Christmas. On Christmas day, Helen was torn between delight at how happy Jeremy was enjoying his Christmas gift and chagrin at being abandoned on one of the premier family days of the year. Little did she realize that it was just a taste of what was to come.

Nothing prepared Helen and Ed for Jeremy's reaction to the

computer and the Internet. Helen was impressed that his seam-less interaction with their computer could actually turn into something more productive than just game playing. Besides, she told herself, computers were the thing of the future. It was an edge for Jeremy, career-wise, to be able to operate a computer so well. Sure, he was spending a lot of time on the computer, but think of all he was learning . . .

As Jeremy's attachment to the machine deepened, Helen grew concerned. Technically, he was progressing beyond what she could have imagined, but he never seemed to have any real friends. Instead of hearing him laughing and chattering in person or over the telephone, the sound of his soft laughter was interspersed with the rapid clicking of the keyboard.

After much discussion, Helen and Ed decided they needed to curb Jeremy's computer time. But how do you tell a teenager you're worried about his social development? Helen thought Jeremy would just become angry. Yet, the more she read about the Internet, the more frightened she became. When she talked to her son about the dangers she was reading about, he just laughed it off. Briefly, Helen thought about just unplugging the thing. But was it really necessary to go that far? After all, Jeremy was a smart kid. He could take care of himself.

Couldn't he?

The Battle for Control

The Internet can be a wonderful tool for kids. Children whose parents do not have the time to take them to the library as soon as each research project comes up at school can find loads of resources on the Internet to help them with reports. They can download charts and pictures to add to otherwise dull papers. They can explore at their own pace and pursue topics that fascinate them. They can tune in to current news stories as soon as they happen and get the weather forecast for the Scout campout next weekend. They can also get involved in things their parents would not want them to get into.

> Children whose parents might not have time to take them to the library can find loads of resources on the Internet.

The older our children get, the more their individual personalities cry out for independence. At the same time, they are still firmly dependent on their parents' care. Since they are so dependent on adults to take care of their needs, they become adept at controlling those adults, thereby controlling their own environment. Often, that means circumventing adult restrictions. And one of the places where children today want to sail free is the Internet. They are exposed to it at school, from their friends, from other adults they know.

So how do you watch over their use of the Internet and enforce restrictions? You quietly, firmly, consistently reiterate two simple rules of life.

Rule #1: The Family Is Not a Level Society

The first rule of a child's life is that you are the parent and he or she is the child. This simple rule illustrates a hierarchy. While growing children will gradually make more and more decisions for themselves, children and parents are not equals in decision making. You, as parent, have the final authority on decisions affecting your children and family—including the use of the family computer, and when and if Net surfing occurs. If this statement makes you feel queasy, take a deep breath. Not all relationships are equal, nor should they be.

You, as the adult, must have a higher position of authority in your relationship for one simple reason: you love your child and are responsible for his or her well-being. You are responsible to your family to produce a productive member. You are responsible to society to produce a contributing citizen. And more importantly, you are responsible to the One who gave you your child to begin with.

There may not be a chapter or verse in the Bible devoted to 24x-speed CD-ROMs or accelerated 3-D graphics cards, but there's quite a bit about raising children. And many of those verses reiterate the concept of parents being the God-given authority over their children. God considered this such a fundamental concept that he included it in the Ten Commandments: "Honor your father and your mother, so that you may live long in the land the Lord your God is giving you" (Exod. 20:12). Verses like this are not to be taken as "gotcha" verses to be thrown out at children in the heat of battle. God considers parenting not just between you and your child; it's his business as well. That child of yours is his child, too. God has given that child to you to love and raise, but God should still be the center of your parenting.

During your years of being a parent, your effectiveness will fluctuate. There will be times when your child will listen intently and follow your instructions without fuss. There will also be times when your children will roll their eyes and do exactly the opposite of what you told them to do.

Parenting can be very trying. It isn't for cowards or quitters. In the face of a determined child's resistance to any sort of control over the Internet, don't give in and don't quit. The Internet can provide a great deal of educational and recreational benefits to your child, as long as you control its use. Don't let its benefits blind you to your need to keep a close eye on its use.

Rule #2: Children Win When They Lose
To win as adults, children need to lose as children. In the battle of wills between parent and child, a child who wins on a regular basis by getting away with inappropriate behavior will really lose as an adult. What is cute and precocious for a two year old is barely tolerated in a seven year old and denounced as rude

and obnoxious in an adult. Whether the issue is how a child behaves online or where a child goes online, Internet use can turn into a test of wills. You need to be the winner now so your child can ultimately win in the future.

Children do not come into this world with an inbred instinct for exemplary, correct behavior. This must be instilled in them by parents who are concerned enough about their welfare to tell them to go to bed when they should, eat their vegetables, and brush and floss daily.

And turn off the computer when they've been on too long.

Parenting Meets Processors

If you are a parent who is concerned enough about your child's use of the computer and the Internet to buy this book, you need to understand that, ultimately, the issue with your child is not about how long he or she is on the computer but who's really in control.

> The issue with your child is not about how long he or she is on the computer but who's really in control.

Does that mean a continual battle of wills, a perpetual all-or-nothing confrontation over your child's computer use? That depends on the level of dependency your child has developed with the computer. The more emotionally tied he or she is to what is being done online, the harder it will be for you to extricate your child from the keyboard and reintroduce him or her to the brave new world offline.

The reason for wanting control over what your child is doing online is the same reason you ask if Billy's parents are going to be home during the party or who's going to be driving to the concert. Just as there are dangers to your child if he or she enters into a situation without parental oversight, there are real dangers on the Internet.

Children do not always perceive danger as a threat to their

well-being. Often, they view danger as adventure and the ability to cope with that danger as proof of their adulthood. Instead of avoiding danger, some children seek it. If your child seeks danger on the Internet, he or she will find it. The Internet can be a very dangerous place, even for adults. Its dangers are magnified when children are involved.

Parental clues are available for all sorts of activities children engage in, from toys to television shows. The Internet, however, is a completely unregulated, mostly unrestricted area. Once a child has gained access to the Internet, information is available, regardless of age. True, many sites warn that their content is for adults only, but these can actually act as beacons for children. And while some pornographic sites can be entered only with the use of a credit card and third-party registration, many sites featuring adults-only content are available without payment. Chat rooms and bulletin boards featuring adult-only themes don't cost either.

On the Internet, basically anything goes. There are images on the Internet no child should ever see. The Internet isn't just made up of harmless, fascinating bits of information and discussion. It is also made up of pornography, pedophiles, violence, sexually explicit graphics, and discussion of

> The Internet is not where you want to leave your child unattended.

deviant behaviors of every kind. This is not where you want to leave your child unattended.

So, what do you do if you believe your child is not being honest with you about where he or she goes on the Internet? You investigate. Remember Rule #1? It has a corollary, which is this: It's your house, including the computer. This is the corollary parents use when they take the step of searching their child's room for pornographic material or illegal drugs. It isn't a step taken lightly by most parents, and it is almost always motivated by love and concern. It's your house; it's your computer, as far as control is concerned. You have the right to investigate that use.

In addition to simply finding out where your child is going on the Internet, you may want to consider parental control software that will help screen out and lock out certain areas of the Internet. (See the Appendix.) There are numerous full service ISPs who have already done the job of screening out objectionable material for you. They also do not allow obscene material through their chat rooms, bulletin boards, or members' Web pages. Of course, nothing is ever 100 percent foolproof; a program that locks out pornography will likely block access to legitimate research about, say, breast cancer.

Maintain a dialogue with your child about her or his Internet experiences. Be an interested and engaged parent. Your children may resist now, but they'll thank you later.

How to Respond

Your perception of how much time your child spends on the computer may be skewed by your fear of what could happen. You may not feel in control when your child is on the computer if your child is much more skilled than you.

Everyone has hobbies, and children are no different. In fact, children spend a lot of time in alternate worlds. Years ago, it was the gunfight at the O.K. Corral, with a red felt hat, a shiny star, and a pair of molded plastic six-shooters in a vinyl holster. Even today, it can be a pile of dress-up clothes, a plastic doll, a sporty toy convertible. What parent ever interrupted their child's imaginary gunfight or the hours spent dressing and combing a doll's hair, saying he or she was spending too much time in that other world? The amount of time your children are on the computer needs to be placed in context with their other activities and their attitudes about the computer.

If you overreact and decide arbitrarily to cut them off completely, chances are your children are going to be upset. They won't understand why you're punishing them. They will become exasperated. Your reaction might be to say, "That's tough!" But while you have God-given authority over your children, you must use it responsibly. The Bible admonishes parents not to embitter their children or they will become discouraged (Col. 3:21). It may be quicker to just blow up and ban them from the Internet, but it won't provide them with the proper training and instruction they need.

Keep Track

Before you confront your child regarding out-of-control computer use, do your homework. Keep track of how much time your child is actually on the computer. When you are home, be aware of when he or she logs on and logs off. If you think your child is spending too much time online while you are gone, try calling home at regular intervals. If you have a phone line just for the computer, call that line. Write down when you tried to call and whether the phone was busy. (Some online services, such as CompuServe and America Online, actually track usage time for you on-screen and can keep running totals. If you subscribe to such a service, find out what steps you need to take to locate this information.)

Too much trouble, you say? By keeping track, you can determine whether your child's computer time is unreasonable. To you, it might appear that your child is always seated in front of the monitor. By keeping track, you can show your child proof of time spent online instead of relying on subjective feelings. If your child does have a problem, indisputable evidence may point out the tendency to deny the problem.

Establish a Schedule and Be Consistent

Sometimes the way to avoid having this constant struggle over the computer is to mutually agree on a set period of time, either a specific amount of time or a specific time span during the day in which your child can enjoy the computer. Together, you agree on the parameters of computer use. But remember Rule #1. Work toward agreement, but if argument persists, you need to assert your authority as the parent and define the parameters of your child's online time.

If you use the computer, consider making up a schedule for the whole family. This will help everyone keep their time straight. Most households today have more

> Consider making up a schedule of computer use for the whole family.

than one television so different family members can watch different programs at the same time. But for most families, buying a second or third computer is not an option. If everyone who uses the computer is part of the schedule, then each family member will know when to use the computer. Have everyone sign off on the schedule; there's something official about signing your name on a piece of paper. Only one caution: You'll have to live up to your part of the schedule.

The schedule removes your tendency to want to play Cyber Cop every time your child logs on. It also removes the constant tension of your child wondering whether you're going to come in angry and demand that he or she "GET OFF THAT COMPUTER!" just as he's about to blast an adversary into galactic space dust.

Once the schedule is agreed on, stick to it, realizing a little give-and-take flexibility will be necessary. Only the military runs on strictly regimented time. But keep to the schedule as much as possible. Mess around with it too much and it becomes meaningless. Be prepared for your child to try to manipulate you to change any schedule to his or her advantage. Don't take it personally. Just stick to your guns and your schedule.

Being consistent also means you may need to take a second look at your own behavior. If you are chastising your child for spending hours on end sitting in front ·of the computer while you spend hours on end sitting in front of the television, be prepared for your child to point out this obvious discrepancy. Your child will probably want to know why he or she is expected to give up online time while you are allowed to continue your hours of television viewing. Perhaps you could arrange for both of you to get out of the house together or with the whole family.

Move the Computer

After you've worked out a schedule, be sure the computer is in a family area of the house. If your child can go into his or her room and shut the door to conduct online activities, there's no way to know what is actually occurring. Even if your child has been given his or her own computer, the bedroom is not the place for it. This is a powerful tool and it needs to be used with supervision.

> **Be sure the computer is in a family area of the house.**

By moving the computer into a common area, such as a family room or kitchen, your child may lose privacy, but he or she will also lose isolation. Most children are social by nature and enjoy spending time with loved ones. Any loss of privacy will be more than made up for by family interaction.

Become Involved

You might also consider taking more of an interest in the computer yourself. Instead of its always seeming to come between you and your child, the Internet can be used as an area of common interest. There are a variety of books available to help even the most entrenched computer novice figure out the basics of the computer and specific software programs. Try enrolling with your child in a class on computers or the Internet. Many recreation departments, city libraries, community colleges, and computer stores offer classes ranging from basic to advanced.

That doesn't mean you have to spend hours on the computer yourself. Just take the time to familiarize yourself with the concepts, vocabulary, and current offerings in cyberspace. When your child comes up for air, he or she will find an informed, engaged ear to tell all about the latest adventure. You may not like the computer that much, but remember, you do love your child.

Consider also that your child might be spending so much time with the computer because you have so little time to spend with him or her. Your child could be using the technology as a substitute for you.

Talk About Online Activities

Unless you plan to sit behind your children and watch exactly what they are doing online, you need to spend time talking with them about their online use. Find out what sites they visit, what online games they play, which chat rooms they frequent, if any, and what sorts of relationships they are forming through those chat rooms or through e-mail. This doesn't need to be done with the equivalent of a cold, metal chair and the glare of bright lights. It's not an interrogation, it's interaction.

Of course, children are not always effusive and completely forthcoming when asked by their parents about their hobbies and daily activities. After six hours or more at school, the question, "So, how was your day today?" is often answered with a discussion-dampening "Fine." Don't give up on the first try if your children don't respond with enthusiasm to your interest in their online activities. Up to this point, the Internet may have been their singular domain. It's their turf and they may not be thrilled about sharing it with you. Be persistent and positive.

If your child is reluctant to discuss what he or she is doing online, there's probably a reason. It could be that your child views your interest as *intrusion* and lack of trust. This may be true if your interest in his or her online activities appears suddenly, without a past history of involvement. While your child may not be happy with your increased interest, be positive yourself and willing to learn. Be reassuring but resolved to monitor your child's online activities. Be patient and stick with it. Be aware also. Maintain your monitoring, even if you are not actually sitting beside your child at all times online. If you suspect your child is going to off-limit areas when you are not present, restrict his or her computer activities to when an adult is physically present.

Be Prepared to Intervene

But what if, through the process of trying to control use of the Internet, your child is adamantly opposed to any reduction in time—or resists any intrusion into his or her online activities? This is a serious problem that needs to be dealt with, not ignored or given in to.

If your child refuses to discuss what he or she is doing online, then you will have to discover other ways to find out. Every computer has an operating system. Whether you use a Mac or a PC, it is not difficult to learn where that computer has gone while online. Every time access to the Internet is gained, the internal memory of the computer knows where you've gone and which sites you had access to. Depending on your operating system, the steps to finding that information will vary. Ask at a local computer store. Call the technical support line for the operating system on your computer. Ask other parents how they know where the Internet has taken their child.

If the problem revolves around the amount of time spent online, any schedule you work out will probably mean less time than your child wants and more time than you're perfectly comfortable with. If you are being reasonable, but feel your child is not, get another opinion. Talk to other parents about how they arrange

> If your child refuses to let you sit in while online, you probably need to find out why.

computer use in their home. Find someone you trust to give you objective feedback.

If you decide your child is not being reasonable, or exhibits any excessively angry, violent, or abusive behavior in response to your boundaries, seriously consider getting professional help. If you have allowed your child free rein on the computer and then, as far as he or she is concerned, inexplicably change the rules, your child may not respond well, initially. But if your child's anger or excessive behavior persists, it could be pointing to a more involved problem.

If your child refuses to discuss what he or she is doing online, there's probably a reason. Wherever your child is going, he or she doesn't want you tagging along. But you need to know. If your child refuses to let you sit in one night while online, you're probably not going to be happy to find out the reason why.

Be Prepared to Set Limits

Err on the side of caution. There is some terrible stuff floating around the Internet, and if your child has gotten hold of it, you need to put an end to it. Immediately. If your child cannot be trusted to use the Internet responsibly at home, consider limiting Internet access. There are public places, such as schools and libraries, where the appropriate portions of the Internet can be accessed. Someone is much less likely to surf to unapproved sites when they're surrounded by teachers and others who are free to glance at their computer screens. (School machines may also be equipped with software that blocks out certain objectionable sites.) Depending on your child and your family situation, restricting Internet use may not be simple or pleasant.

It's not easy to acknowledge that your child has obtained pornography or made friends with an adult in an inappropriate forum. But denial or inconsistent oversight will only further the damage. Keep at it until you either gain control of the situation or find the help you need to reassert your parental authority over your child.

If you feel your child is acting in an inappropriate way, has taken on a substantially different personality, or is secretive about online activities, seek help. At this point, it's really not about the computer. The time online is a symptom of the real problem, whether it is willful disobedience or an addiction to the Internet. If you've done your homework and are convinced your child has a problem, don't stop until you have found out what it is and sought help. Family counselors are available in all price ranges and settings. Pastors and other spiritual leaders are another excellent source of help in family situations. Many churches and synagogues have youth ministers, family counselors, and others who can act as intermediaries. You could find someone who not only offers wise, biblical counsel but who also knows a GIF from a JPEG.

Hobbies are wonderful mini-vacations. You have them, and your child has them. Use common sense in determining whether the Internet is a mini-vacation or a new home-away-from-home. Place reasonable limits on your child's use. Stick with them, even in the face of determined resistance. You're not just thwarting a child; you're molding a responsible adult. Your child will thank you (eventually).

The Next Step

1. Pray for wisdom, courage, strength, and patience. Any time parents deal with children, they need an extra dose of these attributes.
2. For at least thirty days, keep a prayer journal related to your prayers for wisdom, courage, strength, and patience.
3. Look over the suggestions in the "How to Respond" section. Pick out two to work on in the next four weeks.
4. Make a list of people, either other parents or friends, who

could provide you with information on how they handle Internet use.

5. Put this book down and spend some time with your child in one new activity this week.

CHAPTER FIVE

The Computer As Competition:

When Spouses or Kids Take a Back Seat

Andrea silently fumed. Her husband, Tom, had said he'd just be online "for a few minutes." Yeah, right. That was over two hours ago. She'd already cleaned up the kitchen from dinner, folded two loads of laundry, and got their youngest child in the bathtub. Anger fueled her movements as she picked up the dirty clothes and towels from the bathroom floor.

She shook her head, remembering how happy she had been when they'd first gotten the computer. Not that she had planned to use it all that much. Tom was the one who really wanted the thing, but Andrea was happy his latest hobby would be one he could engage in at home. So she hadn't really minded that they'd bought a computer instead of replacing the living room furniture. She figured it was worth a ratty-looking sofa to have Tom at home more.

Her anger waned as she got the kids ready for bed. She was really too tired to put much energy into it, anyway. She stood in the doorway to the den as the kids said good night to their father. He stopped long enough to turn in his chair and accept their hugs and kisses. As soon as they started out the door, though, he swiveled around, intent on the screen again. Andrea's emotions flared again, so she made sure to spend some extra time with each of the kids before they went to bed. It wasn't their fault their father was being a total jerk. Why should they suffer because he was so obsessed with being online?

"How much longer?" she called from the hallway after the lights were out. Her tone of voice made it evident she felt it was far too long already. Tom mumbled an answer and gave her an absent-minded wave with his left hand. The one that wasn't needed on the mouse.

She almost wished he'd take up golf again. At least with golf she knew how long he was going to be gone. With the computer, being home didn't mean the same thing anymore. That is, it didn't mean the same thing to Tom. To her, being home meant being mentally focused on the home, being involved with the family and with family things. To Tom, being home meant physically occupying space in the house. This difference in their viewpoints had been discussed and nit-picked on numerous occasions, with no resolution in sight. This was the worst crisis in their marriage so far.

Time, Energy, Money

Three areas of a marriage can be adversely affected by one spouse's habitual use of the Internet. The first is *time*. There are only a finite number of hours in a day. If your spouse is devoting a great deal of those hours to the Internet, he or she simply has less time available for you. It isn't wrong of you to require time from your spouse. If you didn't want to spend that time, you probably wouldn't have married him or her in the first place.

The second area is *energy*. Just as there are only a finite number of hours in a day, people have only so much energy to put into those hours. If your spouse continues to devote energy to thinking about the computer and about the Internet, even while offline, that energy is being diverted from other things, like working on your relationship. No one puts all of his or her energy into just one relationship, but marriage is certainly one area where energy needs to be expended. Relationships don't just maintain themselves magically, without effort. A marriage requires both time and energy to improve and especially to get over the rough spots. It isn't wrong of you to want your spouse to devote a significant portion of his or her energy each day to the two of you.

> Time, energy, and finances can all be negatively affected by Internet use.

The third area the Internet can negatively affect in a marriage is *finances*. The Internet, and the computer hardware and software required to sustain that connection, requires money. Monetary decisions should be discussed and agreed upon by both parties in marriage. Dissension and division occur when one spouse spends the family money on a pursuit only he or she is interested in. It isn't wrong of you to expect to be consulted and have a say in the amount of money spent to keep the computer upgraded and the Internet connected.

If these three areas are being adversely affected by the Internet, your discussions with your spouse have, no doubt, been emphatic and repeated. You may be ready to just yell and demand your due. While that might be tempting, it is bound to be ineffective.

If you have been left in the dust by your loved one's relentless pursuit of Net Nirvana, realize that you cannot force your spouse to get off the computer and pay attention to you. If you badger, whine, cajole, or otherwise make yourself a nuisance, your spouse will probably pay attention to you in the end—but it won't be the kind of attention that can benefit your relationship.

Attractive Opposites

It is a truism that opposites attract in marriage. Each person seeks out someone to round out his or her own personality. This allows for a wonderful completeness as a couple but can be quite exasperating to live with individually. In the midst of any conflict within marriage, your own viewpoint can obscure the possibility that your spouse may be looking at things from a completely different angle. What may seem logical and obvious to you may seem irrational and obscure to your spouse.

For example, suppose you are the kind of person who finds the absence of the spoken word sheer torture. You automatically assume that if your spouse isn't speaking to you, for whatever reason, he or she must be upset with you. Why else would your beloved rather interact with a box than with you? To you, going online instead of spending time with you is a nonverbal slap in the face. It's personal.

Try looking at it from a different point of view. Your loved one may be the kind of person who doesn't need constant verbal reinforcement to feel connected. The amount of actual conversation she or he needs may be considerably lower than yours. If you constantly judge your spouse, using as a reference the amount of conversation you need, he or she will always come up short. And you'll always feel shortchanged.

You may be the kind of person who loves to share your feelings. You like nothing better than spending an hour discussing a problem or situation from every conceivable angle, picking it apart, and coming up with the best possible solution. The whole process to you is invigorating, energizing. Your loved one, however, may find this activity to have the exactly opposite effect. To him or her, endlessly discussing a problem only elevates the level of anxiety. It isn't energizing; it's exasperating. He or she would rather relax, take a mental vacation from the whole thing, and concentrate on something completely different (like something on the Internet). Then, refreshed, your spouse can come up with an answer to the problem, almost on a subconscious level.

Or maybe you look at the computer and you can't imagine how anyone could spend so much time on it. For you, it's a tool to be used, not a toy to be played with. To your spouse, however, it may not be so cut-and-dried. It's not a necessary evil to be put up with for the sake of modern convenience and time savings. It's a galaxy-spanning vehicle, whose destination is wherever imagination determines. It's information and ideas coming at warp speed. It's not function; it's freedom. The Internet is fun. Why, your spouse wonders, do you constantly want to keep him or her from having fun?

Tom and Shelley

Media reports include horror stories of families who break up because of one spouse's obsession with being online. But every story doesn't have to have an unhappy ending. Many couples have faced the challenge of uncontrolled Internet use successfully. Take the example of Tom and Shelley (not their real names). Until his early thirties Tom had spent his life as a bachelor. He grew up around computers, with an affinity for anything remotely technical. He discovered the Internet in the early nineties and started playing MUDs, the cyber equivalent of role-playing games, before there was even an official designation for them. He graduated from playing MUDs to designing and administering one.

> Many couples have faced the challenge of uncontrolled Internet use successfully.

Tom's work involved computers, and his personal life was

devoted to them. He spent most of his waking hours either working on or playing on computers and the Internet. His friends consisted mostly of other singles, many of whom also were involved with computers and the Internet. His job allowed him flexible hours, so he was able to stay up late and surf the Net. Tom was happy.

Then Shelley moved to town. Shelley met Tom at church, where they sometimes participated in singles activities together. Shelley became very involved with church, and Tom always seemed to be around, fixing one of the church's computers or helping out a member with a computer problem. They began to see a lot of each other. Eventually, they married.

Tom's life used to be consumed with online time. Shelley was used to the one-on-one, intense "together time" of dating. So, how is married life for them now?

Shelley is learning all about computers and the Internet. She has recognized how much Tom enjoys them and is taking an interest in what he considers important. By actively engaging herself in something Tom enjoys, Shelley has ensured that they will have lots of time together and Tom still gets to spend time online. In addition to learning about the computer, she's also learning about Tom. And since she loves Tom, he's her favorite subject!

Tom has found he doesn't spend as much time online as he used to. And, frankly, he says he doesn't miss it all that much. He gave up administering the MUD, though he'll still go in from time to time to play. He realized he spent so much time online when he was single because there wasn't all that much else to do. He can still go a little crazy and spend four hours in front of the monitor without even thinking about it, but that doesn't happen very often. And if it does, Shelley is good about gently reminding him how much time he's spending online and reminding him how good things will be, as soon as he logs off.

How to Respond

If your spouse is spending too much time online, you are not helpless. There are things you can do to change the situation and change your perspective on it.

Consider Your Attitude

It is said that honey attracts more flies than vinegar. When you go to your spouse to explain your feelings regarding his or her Internet use, be aware of your attitude. Demanding, nagging, and whining are not the way to bring about a change in behavior. Those actions may send your spouse straight to the Internet to escape.

How you approach a problem can go a long way toward ensuring its eventual outcome. "A gentle answer turns away wrath, but a harsh word stirs up anger" (Prov. 15:1). This subject has probably already stirred up enough anger within your marriage. Isn't it time to approach your spouse in love and gentleness?

> Make sure your attitude is not contributing to your spouse's desire to escape.

Consider Your Alternative

You want your spouse to get off the Internet. You want your spouse to spend some time with you, talking with you. Consider the kind of alternative you give your spouse to being online. Are you constantly nagging your spouse to get off the computer so he or she can complete your long list of household duties? When you are able to talk to your spouse, is it only about negative things? Do you complain about the neighbors, the kids, your own life, how much time gets spent on the Internet? Is talking to you, is *being* with you, a pleasant experience or something that must be endured? It isn't enough to just want your spouse to get off the computer because he or she is having fun and you're not. Make sure your attitude and the alternatives you present are not contributing to your spouse's desire to escape within cyberspace.

Explain Your Feelings

Make sure there is no communication gap between how you're feeling about the Internet and how your spouse feels about it. Communicate clearly how you feel when your spouse chooses to spend a great deal of time apart from you. Say something like, "When you spend more than an hour in the evening on the Internet, I feel left out of your life," or, "I miss being together with you, talking with you, when you spend every Saturday afternoon surfing the Net."

> Plan a romantic rendezvous at a time when your spouse would normally be online.

If you are going to include the financial end of your spouse's Internet use, be prepared to give exact figures about how much money is being spent. Communicate clearly your feelings regarding how that money is being used. Your spouse may not have realized just how much of your paychecks are going toward the computer and the Internet. Provide the information to illuminate, though, not to browbeat.

Explain that just occupying the same space in the same house is not the same to you as actually being together. Remind your spouse of the type of time and activities you engaged in while dating each other. Remind your spouse of how much fun you used to have together.

Ask your spouse to explain how he or she feels about the amount of time spent online. Allow your spouse the opening to admit that it's gotten a little out of hand. Be gracious and forgiving. Give your spouse positive reasons why he or she should want to forego the Internet to spend more time with you.

Be creative. Plan a romantic rendezvous at a time when your spouse would normally be online.

Do All You Can

The only person you can positively change is you. If your spouse refuses to respond to your requests to curb his or her time on the Internet, you can still work on yourself. Responding to the rebuff with anger, bitterness, and resentfulness will ultimately be more damaging to you. Living day after day with such poisonous negative emotions is not healthy.

Do all you can by giving the effort more than one or two instances to work. If your spouse has a serious Internet dependence, it will take a concerted effort over an extended period of time to reclaim your proper place in his or her life. Please do not give up on your spouse or your marriage. Continue to work on your own attitude and alternatives. Continue to try different avenues to make clear your feelings about his or her online activities. Continue to do all you can to reconnect to your marriage partner. Remember, you vowed for better or for worse. Dealing with your spouse's Internet abuse could definitely fall into the latter category. But when you are able to reconnect, you'll be back in the former.

You may need to seek out a counselor for your situation. Entrenched Internet abuse by your spouse may require more than just your love and concern; it may require intervention. You're trying to salvage a precious relationship, your marriage. Use every avenue at your disposal to help your spouse bring his or her Internet activities under control.

The Next Step

1. Review the last three conversations you've had with your spouse regarding Internet use. List the words you used

and the attitude you displayed. Write out how you could say it differently in the future.

2. Divide a piece of paper into two columns, "Positive" and "Negative." Think about the subjects you routinely discuss with your spouse and write them down in the appropriate column. Review how balanced your communications are with your spouse.

3. Arrange some time alone with your spouse. Plan an activity your spouse finds especially meaningful or fun to reconnect emotionally.

4. Devote time to your spiritual life. If your relationship with your spouse is rocky because of your renewed commitment to curbing his or her online time, you'll need to be spiritually refreshed by the one relationship that will always meet your needs.

CHAPTER SIX

The Threat of Online Relationships:

Intimacy with Strangers

Bill still couldn't quite believe it. The past six months seemed unreal, as if they had happened to someone else. He wished they *had* happened to somebody else. There were times he didn't think he could stand it.

He got up and began to pace the room. Never, in his wildest dreams, did he think he'd lose his wife to someone she met over the Internet. He had never paid much attention to what she did in those chat rooms. He had gone out to work in the yard rather than sitting inside at a keyboard all day long. During the last six months, he had spent a lot of time working in the yard—and she had spent a lot of time online. Now, their lawn was immaculate but their marriage was a mess.

When had things begun to change for them? When had they started to enjoy more things apart than they did together?

It was terrible to learn she had spent all of that time cheating on him in his own home. One night, she angrily had told him all the things she had talked about with her new online "friend." It made his stomach turn. How could she? Why would she?

He guessed it didn't matter much anymore. Not only was she leaving him—saying she just didn't love him anymore, that they had nothing in common anymore—she was leaving him to go live with her new lover in Detroit. Somehow he had been completely replaced in his wife's affections, all because of a casual acquaintance on the Internet that had turned into something else.

He guessed he should just be glad there weren't any children. Yet that seemed to hurt the most. He had been looking forward to beginning a family. Now he was facing the end of one.

Accidental Intimacy

The interactive parts of the Internet—chat rooms, newsgroups, and e-mail—are a tremendous resource. They allow families that are spread across the country or around the world to communicate with each other with minimal expense. A conversation that would take hours of telephone time can be written back and forth and sent via the Internet in just a few seconds. Disabled people who find it tremendously difficult to communicate via the phone or postal service have found in the Internet a method of communication that meets their needs. It can be managed at a time convenient to their schedules, it requires no physical ability other than that of typing, and one can handle it entirely from home.

Nevertheless, while two-way Internet communication is a great blessing to many people, for some it creates an arena for temptation to cross personal boundaries. As you evaluate whether a loved one or friend has become unduly connected to the Internet, be aware that his or her link to the Internet may not be just an activity; it may also be a person. You will need to explore this possibility if the Internet area being abused is one of the two-way arenas: e-mail, newsgroups, and chat rooms.

Two-way Internet activities provide a potent mix of immediacy, anonymity, and intimacy. This combination has the potential to catch a person unaware.

> While two-way Internet communication is a great blessing to many people, for some it creates an arena for temptation.

Due to a misspelled e-mail address, one man received an intriguing message from someone by accident. A relationship was launched by his simple question, "Who are you?" At first, he didn't know if the person on the other end was male or female. All he knew was that he or she was articulate and interesting. The question of gender was soon answered as she, a twenty-three-year-old student, began an extensive, explicit account of her crazy love life. He said it seemed strange at first to be sharing details of such a nature, but he was drawn in by the idea of learning so much about a stranger's life. Intimacies begat intimacies as he responded with details from his own life.

For six months he kept up this relationship, learning bit by bit who she really was. For six months, he was hooked. He looked forward to their time together. After months of correspondence, it still came down to the same question in different forms, "Who are you?" Each message provided another piece of a tantalizing puzzle. She was mysterious, elusive, and, at the same time, remarkably personal in her correspondence.

Then, one day, his wife became curious. She asked about this person he was spending so much time conversing with electronically. The messages were still on his computer, so he showed them to his wife. He figured she'd be mildly interested. Instead, she angrily accused him of having an affair. The thought appalled him. He said that wasn't the case at all. Then why, she wondered, had he not once, in half a year of conversation—much of it personal—mentioned he had a wife and two children? He didn't have a good answer. Shocked, he realized he had allowed a casual, conversational relationship to become a deep, intimate one.

E-mail is not the only arena where relationships can turn inappropriate. Other relationships can start in a public chat room or newsgroup. With the security of a large group of people talking back and forth, relationships can form around a common interest or topic. If users desire privacy, they can establish a personal chat room. The more private the conversation, the deeper the relationship. Enthusiasm for one topic can change into enthusiasm regarding another altogether different and more intimate area. The companionship of ideas has the ability to create a false sense of intimacy in other areas.

How to Respond

There are things you can do, however, to prevent this form of intimacy or to help someone re-establish appropriate personal boundaries when they have been breached by an online relationship.

Shine a Light on It

Sometimes, it is necessary to put a little light on a subject to see it clearly. If you suspect your spouse (or friend or loved one) is engaged in an inappropriate online relationship, make the details of that relationship your business. While you may not know who the other person is, you can certainly know what he or she and your spouse are talking about. Remove the anonymity as far as your spouse is concerned. While a person may be able to conceal his or her identity to the online contact, you do not have to allow such concealment to extend to you. Find out about it. Bring it to light.

Whenever possible, ask your spouse or loved one for a copy of the conversation. If there is nothing wrong with what he or she is discussing, then there should not be a problem with your reading it. Correspondence carried on in a darkened room at three in the morning may have a certain mystique that can be quickly dispelled by reading it aloud in the middle of a sunny day. Shining a light on the conversation can remove a great deal of intrigue and mystery.

Fight for the Family

If the person you are concerned about is a family member whose Internet connections are adversely affecting your family ties, fight to stay together. Your family is worth the effort. If this person is your young child, you have every right to monitor and curtail any relationship begun online that is detrimental either to your child or your family. However, if your child is an adult, your response to his or her Internet relationships may have to take on the tenor of a friend rather than a parent. The only exception to this is if your adult child is using your home and your computer to make inappropriate connections to the Internet. Since this is your property, you have the right to control its use.

Marital relationships especially can suffer significant damage because of the Internet. If the person you are concerned about is a spouse, take action against any relationship that endangers your marriage vows. You have the right to expect fidelity from your spouse's other relationships. You would not tolerate your spouse bringing another person into your home for intimate physical contact. Do not tolerate your spouse bringing someone in for intimate conversational and emotional contact.

Be a Friend

If the person you are concerned about is a friend, it will be more difficult for you to insert yourself into that person's cyber relation-

> Ask what his or her feelings would be if your roles were reversed.

ships. The deeper your friendship, the more likely you will be in a position to probe and determine whether your friend is just hooked on being online or linked to a specific person online. Use your friendship and your concern as a basis for asking those questions.

Talk with your friend about how your friendship has changed and, possibly, diminished because of his or her online activities. Express your desire to renew and strengthen your friendship. Stay in contact with your friend, even if that contact is not reciprocated. You cannot force your friend back into a relationship with you, but you can make yourself available if he or she desires to return.

Ask your friend to see the relationship from your point of view. Ask what his or her feelings would be if your roles were reversed. Given the content of the relationship, how would he or she respond if *you* were the person who was communicating online? Remember the story about the man who began a relationship with a woman online quite by accident? He never intended for the relationship to become what it did. His sense of denial kept him from realizing the damage it was doing. Only his wife's assessment that he was having an affair caused him to reconsider the content of his correspondence.

All of this needs to be done in love and clearly communicated to your spouse, child, or friend. In order to have the courage to break off a compelling online relationship, the Internet user may need the assurance of the strength of your relationship. Give your loved one or friend a loving reason to change, to respond, to re-establish his or her connection to you. You'll both be blessed for the effort.

The Next Step

1. Write a letter affirming your love and explain how the online relationship makes you feel about yourself and your relationship with your loved one.

2. Ask your spouse or loved one to tell you what needs his or her online relationship is meeting. Discuss openly any areas in your relationship that may not be meeting your loved one's needs.

3. Commit to working hard on your end of the relationship. Express your commitment to your spouse or family member.

4. Know that there may be a time when outside help would be advisable. Seek that help if the time comes.

5. Have two willing people pray for you daily for thirty days. Ask them to pray for strength and wisdom regarding how to communicate with your loved one.

CHAPTER SEVEN

Internet Pornography at Home:

When Filth Comes through the Phone Line

M ary prided herself on the precautions she took to protect her family. If the temperature outside was below sixty degrees, everybody went out of the house in a jacket. The children were required to wear safety helmets when they rode their bikes or went skating. They were never allowed to study at the library unattended. She signed them up for classes at the local pool so they would know how to swim. No party invitation was accepted until she had spoken to the adult who was going to be there to supervise. Alcohol was not permitted in her home, and Mary did not smoke; she lectured her children on the dangers of both, frequently. Mary thought she was safe. She thought she had shielded her family from harm.

Her primary concern when she had first purchased the computer was that they would spend too much time on it playing games. She had carefully reviewed every potential game purchase to make sure it was educational first, recreational second. She had absolutely refused to buy the children one of those game systems that operated through the television, but she had given in on a computer. She used one at work and knew how beneficial it could be to the children's studies.

All of her precautions, however, failed to prepare her for the extent of her eldest child's Internet education. He seemed so grown up and mature for his age. She periodically left him in charge of his younger sister and brother if she had to run a quick errand. It was a relief to be able to get away from the house, knowing she could trust him. So the blow came hard when Mary found out she couldn't. She did not know whether to yell or to cry, so she had done both.

After all her preparations and precautions, her son had still gotten into serious trouble. In her own home. She had left him in charge of the kids while she ran to the grocery store. She said she would be back in about an hour. But when she got to the store, she realized she had left her wallet on the dresser, and she had run back home to get it. Since she went into the house the back way, the kids didn't even know she was home. When she walked down the hall past the den, she had seen her son. He was so engrossed in what he was looking at, he didn't even hear her come up behind him.

She was disgusted by what she saw on the screen. She must have made a sound, because her son turned around, the blood draining from his face. Caught. Embarrassed. Ashamed. Frozen. Without a word, she flicked the power off. That was a week ago, and the machine was still off. Of course, that really did not solve the problem. But what was she going to do?

The Back Alley of the Information Superhighway

The number of pornographic sites on the Internet has grown exponentially over the past several years. These include fee-based sites as well as dozens of totally free newsgroups that feature pornographic images—including everything from the "soft-core" *Playboy* centerfold to hard-core images of bestiality, child pornography, fetishes, sodomy, and on and on.

In the free-for-all availability of the Internet lies the potential to bring absolute filth into your house through your computer. Most of you who read this will be determinedly unaware of the kinds of pornography accessible over the Internet. You don't want to see it, and you don't even want to hear about it. But you need to hear about it. Someone in your house may be seeing it.

In a set of articles by the *Seattle Post-Intelligencer,* the newspaper reported that sex is the most searched-for topic on the World Wide Web. So, what happens when you type in *sex* on a search engine? On the Alta-Vista search engine, the search term *sex* will provide a list of over 7 million sites. While not all of these sites are dedicated to pornography, an overwhelming number of them are, with some offering links to live-action pornography. There is no shortage of pornographic sites available on the Internet, with access as easy as typing in a three-letter word.

> On one search engine, the word <u>sex</u> provided seven million sites.

Consider some other statistics about the Internet:

- In the United States, 30 percent of online households will visit an adult Internet site at least once a month.
- Only 4 percent of computers are purchased with any sort of screening software already installed.
- Currently, 19 million children have access to a computer. Almost 10 million children have access to the Internet.
- Some 80 percent of respondents answered yes in a 1997 nationwide telephone survey by Chilton Research Services concerning whether the government should take steps to control access to pornographic material on the Internet to protect children.
- About 25 percent of workplace computers in the United States contain pornography, according to a 1997 study by Digital Detective Services, Inc.

- There is one pornographic site that reportedly receives an estimated 7 million visits ("hits") a day.
- A 1997 *Seattle Times* article about the 24-year-old president of an Internet pornographic empire stated that, according to Forrester Research, the projected online spending for adult entertainment in 1996 exceeded $51 million. Aside from a few specialty sites, adult entertainment was the only fee-based service making any money.

With millions of sites to choose from, there is pornography of every kind on the Internet. You don't need to go looking for pornography on the Internet, either. Without even trying, many people have found it staring them in the face. The problem is so serious that the U. S. Customs Service has a tip line where you can report child pornography on the Internet (send e-mail to cybersmuggling@customs.sprint.com).

You Can't Tell a Site by Its Link

Not everyone who visited a pornographic site on the Internet did so intentionally. Pornographic sites are becoming more and more ingenious in how they appear on search engines so as to snag users unaware. Unfortunately, many of those caught are children.

According to the report by the *Post-Intelligencer,* a search on the Webcrawler search engine for the term *kitty* brings up a site called Persian Kitty, a pornographic link. The Persian Kitty link provides access to about a thousand adult links which advertise their content through graphic, illustrated teasers. Searches for *toys, Bambi, wrestling,* and other topics children might look

> Not everyone who visited a pornographic site on the Internet did so intentionally.

for can lead them inadvertently to pornographic material.

A colleague went online to do research regarding a recent advertising campaign by a national trade association. He found what he was looking for—and something he wasn't. As he was searching related sites, he came upon a graphic picture of a well-endowed woman only partially dressed. He made a mental note to be even more careful about which sites he chose to view.

When NASA's Pathfinder landed on Mars in July 1997, millions of people hopped onto the Internet, eager to view the stunning visual images beamed back to earth. What some of them saw could be termed *earthy*. NASA's information was at nasa.gov. However, anticipating the interest, a pornographic Internet company made a new destination, nasa.com. When unsuspecting viewers mistakenly typed *nasa.com* in the address bar of their browser, they were routed to the pornographic site and saw a video stripper.

Pedophilia and Child Pornography

Possessing or transmitting child pornography in the United States is against the law. But the Internet is still loaded with illegal pornographic images of children. Part of the problem is the mobility inherent on the Internet. If a kiddie-porn site is discovered and closed down, the operators will simply move, choose a different name, and start up business somewhere else on the Net. They can quickly change identities and addresses. Keeping up with them is difficult. Although federal law enforcement agencies are infiltrating Internet pornography rings that feature children, most law enforcement agencies are woefully understaffed and inadequately trained to keep track of pedophiles and child molesters who have taken up residence on the Internet.

Compounding the problem is the number of child pornography sites that originate outside of the United States. There are an estimated five thousand of them. Not all countries have laws prohibiting child pornography, and those that do are not currently any better equipped to deal with this problem than their U.S. counterparts. At this point, the law breakers have a tremendous advantage on the Internet over the law enforcers.

All of this means you cannot be complacent about what images get downloaded to your home computer. Societal, established barriers are not yet in place. You will need to establish your own.

The danger to your child is not confined to visual images. Pedophiles (those who sexually abuse children) have moved to the Internet to find fresh victims and to communicate with each other regarding their victims. In one recent incident, an eleven-year-old girl met a man in an Internet chat room. They exchanged phone numbers and agreed to meet. This young girl was subsequently raped by her thirty-six-year-old "friend."

> **Pedophiles and child molesters have moved to the Internet.**

Molesters and pedophiles find their victims through chat rooms specific to children and through online games. They pose as children themselves and engage children in conversation. Before long, the conversation turns to how the child feels about him or herself, the child's family, and the child's physical appearance. According to Detective Michael Sullivan, an investigator with the Naperville, Illinois, Police Department's Internet Crimes Unit, before the Internet, pedophiles targeted children in parks and playgrounds, offering candy to build their trust. Now, in the virtual park of cyberspace, they offer conversation and personal questions to determine whether they can lure the child into sexual discussions. The danger posed by pornographic material on the Internet has an incredible impact on children who are ill-prepared to cope with its substance or with manipulation by adults whose goal is to cause them harm.

Traps and Snares

While children are certainly at risk from this pornographic material, they are not the only members of the family who can fall prey to its lures. If you are in a family, you should not only be aware of the danger to your children, but also to yourself and/or the adult males in your household. The overwhelming majority of adults who voluntarily view and seek access to pornographic material are men. (For a more comprehensive discussion, please see chapter 10.)

Pornography on the Internet can entrap Internet users quickly. It is abundant and easy to find. It is private. Sexual fantasies are the stuff of these Internet sites, with every conceivable fantasy represented. The variety of pornographic images and sexual conversations provide an overwhelming array of temptations for even the most disciplined individual.

I know of a minister, a very spiritual man, who once worked with teenagers. He became concerned over the potentially damaging images his church kids could have access to on the Internet. So he decided to investigate just how easy it would be to gain entry to pornography online. He was doing it to keep up-to-date with the temptations and trials his teenagers were facing. As an adult and a spiritual leader, he assumed he would be immune from what he found. He wasn't.

Increasingly, he found more and more of his time being devoted to his "research." He started out in what he thought was a controlled manner. Then he kept telling himself he could quit anytime, but he never seemed to get around to it. He began to visit more graphic sites and intensified his viewing, particularly of homosexual erotica. Soon, all of his pornographic viewing was homosexual in nature. Before long, just viewing other men wasn't enough. While telling others at church that he was counseling or running errands, he began to frequent gay bars looking for men to engage in sex. When the truth became known, his ministry was demolished, his marriage shattered, his career destroyed.

There is simply too much damage to be done to your family by Internet pornography. It is predatory, pervasive, and persistent. Do not automatically assume it could never happen in your home.

How to Respond

You are not helpless in dealing with this, however. There are a number of steps you can take to protect yourself and your family.

Protect Your Children

The following list of suggestions has a variety of sources, including the National Committee to Prevent Child Abuse, the National Center for Missing and Exploited Children, Childwatch, and America Online.

- Keep the computer in a common area of the home, such as the living room or kitchen, where activity on the Internet can be monitored. Do not allow it in your child's bedroom.
- Do not use the Internet as a baby sitter. Know where your child goes online.
- Explain to your children that they are never to give out personal information to anyone online, even if they feel they know them. Children are never to give out their real last name, e-mail address, home address, telephone number, or the name of their school without your express permission.

- Become familiar with whom your child is conversing in a chat room, even if those chat rooms are for children. The "child" your child is conversing with could be a predator.
- Screen e-mail. View any and all attachments sent to your children. These could contain pornographic images.
- If your child is allowed to go online while you are not home, use a filtering program.

One word of caution regarding filtering programs. They are not a perfect solution. *Consumer Reports* magazine tested four of the largest Internet filtering programs: SurfWatch, Cyber Patrol, Cybersitter, and Net Nanny. They chose to test the four with twenty-two easily obtained objectionable Internet sites. Four sites got past SurfWatch. Cyber Patrol failed to screen out six of the sites. Cybersitter missed eight, and, amazingly, Net Nanny did not screen out a single one. Filtering technology will undoubtedly get better, but nothing can filter out objectionable material better than your concerned vigilance.

> Nothing can filter out objectionable material better than your concerned vigilance.

Protect Your Relationships

No matter who in your house is entering the Internet, be aware of what is happening online. If a friend or family member has a problem, it may be up to you to bring that problem to light. This is especially true if the person having a problem is your spouse. If your spouse has become addicted to Internet pornography, he or she is going to need all of your compassion, strength, and determination to overcome this difficult obsession. But you cannot begin to help him or her deal with the problem if you don't even know it exists.

You cannot be ambivalent about this activity. You must be clear and specific regarding your opposition to your spouse's continuing this activity. If he or she reads nothing else in this book, insist that he or she read chapter 10. Add your own feelings and observations to those made in that chapter. Make it personal. Be persistent in monitoring your spouse's online viewing and seek professional counseling for you both. One spouse's dependency on Internet pornography can have a devastating effect on both of you.

The Next Step

1. Get close. To ascertain whether someone close to you has a problem, you have to be close and attentive. If your daily activities or current feelings have caused you to operate at a distance from someone you love, begin today to close the gap. Do whatever you need to do to reconnect with your loved one. Forgive. Apologize. Cut down on your activities. Do less. Listen more.

2. If the person you're concerned about is your child, determine today to follow the guidelines suggested earlier. Remain informed about dangerous trends that might affect your child on the Internet. Do further research. (Be sure to look over the Additional Resources section at the end of this book.)

3. You are not in this alone. You have an advocate in your quest to rid your home and your family relationships of Internet pornography. God also wants this activity to be banished from your home. Spend time in prayer, asking for his strength and guidance.

4. Consider switching to an Internet Service Provider that filters pornographic sites. Though this is not fail-safe, it is an important step.

5. Get help. There are counselors who can assist you. Ask a pastor for a recommendation, seek out a community

agency, look up counselors through a professional group such as the American Association of Christian Counselors, or call the phone number for The Center at the back of this book.

SECTION TWO

FOR THE ONLINE USER

CHAPTER EIGHT

Do I Really Have a Problem?

Making a Self-Assessment

Bob looked up at the clock and was amazed at what he saw: 2:15! Where had the time gone? He had just sat down to e-mail some friends and check out a Web site or two. That was four-and-a-half hours ago. He silently cursed himself, shaking his head. He had planned on being online for only an hour at most. He had a presentation at work early tomorrow—no, today! He could feel his body and mind sagging with fatigue. He would have to get into bed immediately and hope four hours of sleep would be enough.

Unfortunately, this wasn't the only day this week that he had lost track of his time online. And with each hour of sleep lost, it was harder and harder to get up in the morning and find the motivation for work. He couldn't keep doing this. The presentation was important to his company and he had lobbied hard to get it. Now, he was not only going into it sleep-deprived, but he really should have spent some time adding a few finishing touches. Now he would have to show it as-is and hope it was good enough.

Bob got up from the computer and stumbled to bed, joining his wife who had been asleep for hours. As he drifted off, he felt a twinge of guilt at coming to bed after she was asleep and leaving the house before she would awaken the next morning. He had a vague sense of unease and drowsily renewed his commitment to keep better track of his Internet time.

He awoke to the sound of the telephone. It was his boss calling—and Bob was fifteen minutes late for the meeting.

It Could Happen to You

None of us likes to admit we have a problem. Most people would rather deal with the ramifications of a bad habit than admit it's a problem—at least, until the consequences begin to intrude dramatically into our personal lives. Certain types of people are especially prone to Internet dependence. It is important to understand who they are and whether or not you may be susceptible.

College Students and the Internet
For most students, a free, school-provided Internet account is a great learning tool. It puts them in touch with other educational institutions, libraries, and museums, providing a vast pool of information to be used in their academic pursuits. For them, the benefits of the Internet are so thoroughly recognized that schools now provide Internet use as readily as they do access to the on-site library.

> Some students give up meals, forego social events, and deny themselves sleep to dwell in a digitized world.

However, at institutions of higher learning all over the country, school officials have become concerned over the amount of time some of their students are spending on non-school activities on the Internet. These students give up meals, forego social events with real people, and deny themselves sleep in order to dwell within a digitized world.

Writing in the journal *CyberPsychology and Behavior,* University of Maryland professor Jonathan J. Kandall notes that this abuse of the Internet has some institutions opening up counseling centers to help students cope with their inability to self-limit their online time. The University of Maryland at College Park, the University of Texas at Austin, Marquette University, and countless others now have such centers. Additionally, according to the article, the University of Washington has instituted a limit on Internet time available to their students.

Are you a student with an Internet account who can't seem to meet your other commitments because of online use?

Hungering for an Adult Voice

Those who stay at home and have a flexible schedule are also susceptible to Internet abuse. It begins with using the Internet as a way to overcome the isolation felt by those who work at home. Removed from much adult contact, perhaps having contact only with children, these individuals rely upon the Internet to feel connected to life outside. The problem comes when this Internet connection becomes a consuming activity.

Such was the case for a Cincinnati woman named Sandra Hacker. According to news reports, she is accused of locking her three children in a room so she could go online without interruption. Police found the children in that room, along with broken glass, debris, and handprints of their feces on the wall. Her husband, from whom she was separated, turned her in to the police. Her children, ages two, three, and five, were taken into police custody after their condition was discovered.

In Umatilla, Florida, Pam Albridge lost custody of her two children, ages seven and eight, after a judge decided she was addicted to the Internet. Custody of the children was given to her husband, Kevin, after he wrote in his petition that his wife is "for want of a better term, addicted to the Internet and ignores the needs of the children." According to testimony during the custody battle, Mrs. Albridge moved the computer into her bedroom after she and Mr. Albridge separated. She put a lock on the door and began to spend most of her waking hours online.

Are you someone who stays at home, only to find yourself spending an increasing amount of time on the Internet, neglecting other responsibilities?

The Unemployed or Underemployed

One of the dangers of the Internet is its ability to fill time with interesting, compelling activity. For those individuals who have no job or who work part-time, the remaining hours of the day can get sucked up into Internet use.

For these people, the Internet becomes a place of significance. Online, making contact is all that matters. Since so much Internet interaction can be anonymous, whether or not someone has a job—or what that job is—is irrelevant.

> Those who are lonely or bored can have problems with Internet abuse.

Being unemployed or underemployed can result in positive Internet use. Time can be spent online gleaning business and career information, making contacts, carrying on conversations. On the other hand, overuse or inappropriate use of the Internet can drain away time and effort without producing anything with which to pay the bills.

Has your time away from work become diverted into an ever-expanding black hole of Internet use?

All or Nothing

There are some people who approach new experiences with abandon. They are all-or-nothing people who tend to go overboard on new pursuits. It's the guy who sets up a darkroom in the basement laundry room after shooting three rolls of film on his first 35mm camera. It's the woman who has more craft projects lined up to do than time left on this earth to complete them. For these people, the motto is this: Anything worth doing is worth doing to the extreme. About the only thing that saves them from becoming totally inundated is the fact that though their pursuits are intense, they are generally short-lived. These people flit quickly from hobby to hobby.

The Internet can be a hobby, but it also provides opportunities to jump from subject to subject—hobby to hobby, if you will—and still stay online. The speed and variety of the Internet can prove an almost irresistible draw to some people. And there is little likelihood that they will give up the Internet altogether, as opposed to merely finding another place or activity online.

Have you gone head over heels with this new medium, allowing your Internet use to become the top priority in your life?

Assessing Your Own Level of Interest

Internet abuse, of course, is not restricted to just these types of individuals or life situations. Anyone can find himself or herself spending more and more time online, without being able to self-limit use.

One of the most common defenses people use when confronted with a personal problem is to laugh it off and suggest that it's not really all that bad. What could be wrong, after all, with the search for knowledge? Or communicating with friends and family? Or getting together with people who like the same things as you do? Nothing. The problem is a matter of degree. To what degree have these online activities taken over other areas of your life? To what degree are these activities having a negative effect on the people around you? To what degree are you unable to moderate your behavior?

Take a look at the following statements, some serious, some humorous. Ask yourself how close to the mark these are for your life.

- You communicate with people on other continents more than you do with the folks next door.

- You promise yourself once an hour that you'll only stay online for another 15 minutes.

- You stay up late waiting for your spouse and children to go to bed so you can go online.

- Everyone you know asks why your phone line is always busy.

- You get up before the sun rises to check your e-mail, and you find yourself in the very same chair again long after the sun has set.

- You buy a pager so family and friends can get through to you.

- You respond immediately to e-mail, while ignoring your growing pile of "snail" mail.

- You sit down at the computer right after dinner and your spouse says, "See you in the morning."

- You're constantly yelling at your spouse for using the phone for stupid things—like talking.

- You brag to your friends about your date Saturday night—but don't tell them it was in a chat room.

- You get more excited about getting an e-mail than a phone call or letter.

- You have a GPA of under 2.5 but you still read newsgroup postings for hours the night before an exam.

- You find yourself brainstorming for new subjects to search on the Web.

- You wake up at three in the morning to go to the bathroom and check your e-mail on the way back to bed.

- You decide to stay in college an additional year or two just so you can keep your free Internet access.

- Every time you press the Get Mail button—you do.

- The remote to your TV is missing, and you don't care.
- All of your friends have an @ in their name.
- You're incensed because your ISP considers unlimited use to be under 200 hours a month.

> Do you wake up at three in the morning to go to the bathroom and check your e-mail on the way back to bed?

All of these items came from various Internet sites dealing with Internet addiction. You may have chuckled when you saw one that really pegged you. And you may be tempted to laugh off this entire discussion as "no big deal." But if you identified with several of the statements, this *is* a big deal. It is likely that you've developed a dependence on your Internet activities. Check out the next list to see if that's the case.

Who Is in Control?

To weigh the significance of your Internet involvement, respond true or false to the following statements for yourself:

- I feel preoccupied with the Internet, thinking about it while offline.
- I feel a need to use the Internet for longer and longer periods in order to achieve satisfaction.
- I can't always control my Internet use.
- I feel restless or irritable when I try to cut down or stop Internet use.
- I use the Internet as a way of escaping from problems or relieving a bad mood.
- I've had to lie to family members or friends about the extent of my involvement with the Internet.

- I've risked the loss of a relationship, job, educational or career opportunity because of the Internet.
- I keep logging on, despite spending more than I would like to on access fees.
- I feel depressed or anxious when I'm offline.
- I stay online longer than I originally planned.

If you can identify with more than four of these, then keep reading. If you feel ready to look at how you are using the Internet, consider how your experience coincides with that of other Internet users who have had to come to terms with their online use.

Surfing with the Sharks

Journalist Joan Connell, reporting on her own Internet addiction for MSNBC, mentioned that she regularly trolled for news on the Internet "like a shark scenting fresh blood." If you approach the Internet determined to learn everything you can about a certain subject, the volume of information can be daunting. It's kind of like painting the Golden Gate Bridge in San Francisco: Once you've reached the end, you have to turn around and start all over again because in the time it took you to do it, what was once new and impressive became old and faded.

E-mail Mania

Are you someone for whom e-mail has become a necessity for a happy life? Unsure? If someone doesn't respond for days, do you begin to wonder, "Why haven't they responded? Was it something I said? Am I not important to them anymore?" And if you don't respond immediately, do you wonder if they are thinking the same thing about you?

If e-mail is your life, you may sincerely expect near-immediate responses from those people you communicate with. Even a delay of one day can produce doubt and anxiety. So this wonderful time-saving device, which was supposed to make life easier, can actually contribute to your stress level, compelling you to spend time relieving that stress by responding to any and all messages.

Face-to-Face Online

Maybe your preferred area of the Internet is a newsgroup or chat room. If so, you have found a forum where you can conduct two-way communication with people all over the world.

If you have a favorite chat room you frequent, you have an expectation of who is going to be there. And you know they expect you to be there as well. Quite possibly, you have told your cyber buddies about the other chat rooms you visit. Maybe you run into these same people in a variety of areas. They're your friends, the ones you open up to, the ones who really understand how you think. They're like family. Sometimes they're even more like family than your real family.

Let the Games Begin

For some, online time is taken up by hopping into a gaming zone on the Internet and turning into an all-powerful wizard or a galactic terror. The Internet has heightened the experience you receive on television-based gaming systems by supplying living, breathing opponents to test your skill. On the other end of the demon you just annihilated with an incantation or the starship you just bested in an interplanetary space duel is somebody just like you, sitting in front of his or her computer. Just like you—except, you're better! The whole thing is fun, exciting, competitive. You can play for hours and not even realize it. The combination of imagination, competition, and online connection is a potent mix.

When Appreciation Turns to Addiction

So what do you do if you're hooked on Net surfing, e-mail, newsgroups, chat rooms, or online gaming? There is nothing inherently wrong with any of these activities. Net surfing is an entertaining way to learn about everything from current events to ancient history. E-mail is a wonderful way to keep up with family and friends. Newsgroups provide contact with people who share your same interests, not unlike being a member of a garden or book club. Chat rooms offer an immediate connection with like-minded people you would never otherwise meet. Online games are entertaining diversions. In and of themselves, these activities aren't bad or wrong.

> E-mail is a wonderful way to keep up with family and friends.

But if, after honest evaluation, you believe you have a problem with Internet abuse, the time to do something about it is now. Somewhere along the line, you have formed a false impression of the Internet. The idea has developed that life as you want it will end if you stop logging on. Note that I didn't say "life as you *know* it." Unless you are suffering from delusions, you will recognize that a life, a reality, exists outside of your Internet use. But this false "life as you *want* it" understanding is compelling you to remain engaged in online behavior that increasingly separates you from the reality of life offline. Ultimately, it is destructive to you and to those around you.

Compare Internet addiction with compulsive gambling—the idea that just around the corner lies something better, something to make everything all right again. Instead of trying to win the next pot or hit the lottery, the goal is to find that one bit of information that makes you a valuable commodity, that sets you apart. It's the thrilling tension of wondering who you'll find to talk to and what you'll have to talk about. It's the fear that if you don't log on, you'll be missing something vital. It's the reality-thwarting thrill of being someone else online.

Gaining the Proper Perspective

The cure for an obsessive activity like this is perspective, the ability to put the activity into the proper context with the rest of your life. If you are a student, there's nothing wrong with hopping on the Internet in your free time for your own enjoyment. But remember that you have educational obligations, probably employment obligations, perhaps family obligations. These obligations need to be weighed against the amount of time you're giving to the Internet—or any other activity. If the Internet has become the most important thing you do all day, your perspective needs to change.

If you're in a relationship with another person or within a family unit, you have obligations to invest time and energy to maintain those relationships. They should have a greater priority in your life than the Internet. If you are constantly putting off being with family in order to spend time online, you are elevating the value of being online and devaluing the people who should be most important to you.

And what about your obligation to yourself? The Internet is a wonderful way to enhance your life. But if your use of it is more like a weight around your neck, it's time to recognize that fact and take steps to change it. A self-imposed down time might be the answer. It worked for Kathy Ruthowski, who wrote in her *True Confessions of Life after Internet Addiction:*

> Recently, I took some time away from the Internet, a moratorium on e-mail, Web surfing, and gophering to spend more time with my family living a life off of cyberspace. One evening I simply turned off my computer and almost instantly felt liberated. I enjoyed spending

time interacting with my children, mother, and husband. I actually read entire books and started a stage play using a pen and legal-sized tablet of paper. I took time to day-dream and walk the dog. It was pleasant not to be staring at a computer monitor and checking my many electronic mailboxes for the latest arriving messages at 1 A.M. In fact it was so pleasant to be away from the onerous demands of cyberspatial interaction that I almost considered pulling the plug permanently. . . . I realized, however, that I had real friends in cyberspace whom I wanted to hear from and communicate with, and without the Internet my ability to stay in touch would be compromised. I also realized that the Internet offered me access to information and knowledge that I would not otherwise have and the ability to reach a larger audience through online publishing. I accepted that my personal challenge would be to learn how to better use this technology in my personal and professional life.

How to Change

Putting things in perspective is the challenge for all of us. There isn't a one-size-fits-all answer to that challenge, either. But here are some practical suggestions.

Track Your Time
Keep track of the actual amount of time you spend online; it may be more than you think.

Keeping a log may seem burdensome, but having to actually record the amount of time you're spending online may be revealing. And as the log becomes an accountability tool, you may voluntarily decide to cut back on your online use. In fact, many diet programs are successful partially because they require participants to keep track of every bite eaten. When confronted with having to write down 428 calories for that chocolate-covered doughnut, a lot of people opt for two carrot sticks and half an apple.

> Having to actually record the amount of time you're spending online may be revealing.

While you're keeping track of online time, track the time you spend on other things as well. Compare the amount of time you spend on the Internet with other worthwhile activities in your life. How does it compare to the amount of time you spend with your children? your spouse? How does it compare to the amount of time you spend doing other things that are important to you, such as exercising, studying the Bible, reading that bestseller everyone's talking about?

In the Bible, Jesus is very clear that we cannot serve two masters. We will always end up loving one and hating the other. Has your Internet use gotten so out of hand that you resent having to go to bed Saturday night so you can get up for church on Sunday morning? Do you forego a church activity so you can be home for a scheduled online chat with a celebrity? By keeping track of the time spent in all of your life's activities, the answers will become very clear.

Take a Walk

If you find yourself sitting at the computer desk for hours, get up and get out. While you're out taking a walk, spend the time thinking about what needs your Internet use fills. What void in your life are you trying to fill up with the computer? Is it a void God should be filling instead?

There's something about being outside, walking at a steady rhythm, that also invites self-evaluation. Being outside in God's creation often helps people draw closer to God and gain his perspective on their "inside" time.

Get Family Input

Ask family and friends for their reactions to your computer use. Talk to your family about what would be a good amount of time for you to be on the Internet. They benefit from your strengths and suffer from your weaknesses. If one of your weaknesses is a compulsive need to be online, your family is suffering because of it. Listen to them. Have them tell you what it feels like when you reject time with them to spend time online.

Ask for their forgiveness, and then experience it. One of the most beneficial family bonding times is when a family member confesses to the rest of the family and receives forgiveness. Pray together about your struggles. Allow family members to help remind you when you take that occasional step backwards. Allow their love for you and desire to be with you to act as accountability tools for your Internet use.

Set a Schedule

With a schedule in place, you and the people around you will know when you're going to be online and for how long.

Reconnect after Disconnecting

Engage in some relational activity after you've logged off. In other words, don't go from the computer to your bedroom and then shut the door. Spend time talking with your family or friends, playing with

> Disconnecting from the Internet may require more than just walking away from it.

your children, reconnecting with loved ones.

When You're Off, You're Off

Mentally disconnect from the computer when you're offline. It won't do you or your family much good if you're physically disconnected from the computer but thinking about the Internet all the time you're off.

Disconnecting from the Internet may require more than just walking away from it. It's not unlike the parable Jesus told in the Gospel of Matthew about the man whose evil spirit left him and then returned. The problem was that the man had found nothing to take the spirit's place once it left, so the room was still waiting when the evil returned. In fact, the Bible states that, if the evil spirit finds the house emptied out, it will return with seven other spirits more wicked than itself. In other words, it's not enough to empty your mind of the Internet, you also need to fill up your mind with positive, engaging thoughts. The chances of your feeling compelled to return immediately to the computer will be diminished if your time away is being used wisely and constructively.

Take Up Another Hobby
Find something new to do that does not involve the computer or the Internet. Make sure the most significant interaction you have with people on a daily basis isn't online.

Be Honest
If you find you're using the Internet to escape from your life, to act as a sort of white noise for inner anxiety, find someone to talk with about it. Initially, depending upon the degree of what you discover, talking to a friend, family member, or other confidante may be just what you need.

Gain Access to God's Perspective
Depending upon the depth of your Internet use, the previous suggestions may prove to be only a first step. The encroachment of the Internet into your personal life may require more than just a simple realization that you've allowed things to get a little out of hand. It may require more than just a surface decision to start doing things differently.

The cure is perspective. But whose perspective do you use if yours has been compromised by your Internet activity? Your family and friends may be so fed up with your behavior that they are ready to tell you to either pull the plug or take a hike. So, whose perspective do you use? Whose perspective will be unbiased and take into account what you want, along with knowing what level of activity is really best for you? Who could possibly know all of that?

God knows. You cannot trust your own perspective on your behavior, so trust his. He knows you, your situation, what makes you tick. And he loves you. Ask him to guide you in determining how much of a problem your Internet use has become and what steps you need to take to bring yourself back into balance.

Of course, many professional, Christian counselors are available to talk with you about your Internet use, if you decide that's a step you need to take. Be sure to find one who understands the Internet and is aware of the research on Internet dependence and abuse.

The Next Step

1. Write down the areas of the Internet you suspect you may be having trouble with. Estimate the amount of time you're spending on the World Wide Web, Usenet, chat rooms, e-mail, and online games.

2. Review the list of responses to "Who Is in Control?" Circle any that really struck a chord for you.

3. Write down what your first response would be if told that you would not be able to go online for a day, a week, a month, or ever again.

4. If Jesus could sit down at a computer today and hop onto the Internet, how do you think he would use it? List ten things Jesus might do on the Internet.

5. Since God is all-knowing, how do you think he feels about

the way you are using the Internet? Ask God to reveal to you the truth concerning your Internet use. Then be prepared to hear the reply.

CHAPTER NINE

E-mail, Bulletin Boards, and Chat Rooms

A New Kind of Importance

Jimmy kept looking at the clock on the wall. *Does class have to be so incredibly boring?* he thought. *I want out! This guy knows nothing. His material must be at least twenty years old. Right now, there's a world moving hundreds of megahertz faster than this guy. Speaking of which, I wonder what I've missed since I logged off?*

Whew! I'm tired. I probably shouldn't have stayed online so late last night—or, rather, early this morning—but there was just so much e-mail to go through. And what about my newsgroups? The stuff we talk about there is actually relevant. Not like this droning professor. Is he ever going to shut up?

I'd love to flame him, but I can't really do that. At least, not here. But I'll be able to let loose tonight in the computer lab.

The Lure of Online Community

For some people, the lure of the Internet is its connection to other people, other places, and information that is literally up-to-the-minute.

The One with the Most Messages Wins

A lot of children love to be the first one to the mailbox. Some-times—amidst the catalogs, magazines, and boring-looking bills—there's even a letter just for them.

Remember how that felt? Somewhere, somebody wanted to talk to you. Just you. It probably made you feel grown up and important. Nobody could open that letter except you. Sure, maybe it was just an ad for some toy you didn't care about. Maybe it was a big, colorful catalog of novelties and joke gifts. But sometimes it was a letter from that kid you met at camp, or your cousin in St. Louis, or your uncle who never seemed to get around to writing anybody else in the family but you.

Now you're an adult and most of the stuff you get in the mail is either junk or all those boring-looking bills. It's not special anymore. Most of it gets trashed or recycled with barely a second look. The trip to the mailbox has lost a lot of its luster.

E-mail, on the other hand, is the treasure-trove of our youth, programmed for the next century. Open up your e-mail and there they are, just like you remember: messages just for you, written by family and friends and even people you don't know. Somehow, even junk e-mail is worth looking at. Bold, important, begging to be read and paid attention to. Each message is like an affirmation of your importance as a person. After all, if you weren't important, would someone take the time to send you a message? And the more messages you have, the more important you are. Isn't that how things work?

> E-mail is the treasure-trove of our youth, programmed for the next century.

What about sending your own message? It is so quick and easy. Open up your address book, choose a recipient, and let the words flow through your fingertips. There's something so satisfying about dashing off an electronic masterpiece and clicking the Send button. And if it's enough of a masterpiece, why stop with just one person? Why not "cc:" five, ten, twenty others?

Read a Good Posting Lately?

But maybe e-mail isn't your thing. Maybe most of the conversations you conduct on the Internet are in specialized areas, such as a bulletin board or newsgroup. You're not just reading a single message from someone, you're perusing hundreds of messages, weighing their value, evaluating their worth, critiquing their style and content. Feel combative? Flame to your heart's content. Feel puckish? Leave irrelevant, irreverent messages. Feel zealous? Rally hundreds of troops to your latest cause. So much freedom. So much influence.

Your fellow Netizens come to know you by the content of the messages you post and the style of your writing. You can hardly wait to see if anyone you recognize has found your posting and replied. Give and take. Back and forth. Thrust and parry. Verbal combat conducted on a global scale—and all on the familiar turf of your favorite subject or topic. What could be better?

Same Net Time—Same Net Channel

For many Internet users, the only "better" is to enter a favorite chat room. There, you don't need to be kept waiting for a response. Instantaneous verbal tit for tat. You can either be surprised by whoever else is in the chat room when you enter, or you can set up a specific time and/or day to meet with others. It's kind of like heading out with friends for coffee in the afternoon. It's relaxing, free-wheeling, and fun.

You come to feel as if you really know these people and they know you. After all, you've talked about all kinds of things. You feel part of a group, connected to the other people online. You speak the same language. You share a lot of the same pet peeves. You're not alone.

Finding Connection, Influence, and Significance

Whether you are struggling with overuse of e-mail, bulletin boards, or chat rooms, the issue is really about creating a sense of connection, influence, and significance for yourself. These are worthy goals. But imagine what life would be like if these pursuits were taken to the extreme with the aid of the Internet.

A man in his early thirties has had any number of jobs over the past five years, but just can't seem to keep them. Whether he's working or not, his main goal in life is to hold on to his Internet connection. If he's broke and has to sell his possessions to make ends meet, he'll find somebody else's computer to get online. As soon as he gets another job and saves up some money, the first thing he replaces is his computer.

He is intelligent and articulate. However, he is also abrupt and blunt. This makes him an interesting and provocative Internet correspondent. Unfortunately, it makes him less than desirable as an employee, especially where the public is concerned. Maybe that's why he has trouble holding down a job.

He sees things in black or white—never in a shade of gray—and he's not reticent to express his views. He likes to adopt causes and rigorously defend them to any and all comers. His ability to argue for his latest purpose in life online is very important to him. He feels the Internet is a way for him to get his argument across to a large number of people.

Since he cannot keep a job, he's always starting at entry level. He rarely stays long enough to progress within a company. Subsequently, at work he is most often told what to do instead of being asked for his opinion. His compliance is expected and his expertise unused.

In order to maintain his sense of connection, influence, and significance, he has traded in normal relationships with people offline. Now, he has allowed his health to suffer by sitting for long periods of time every day, eating quick, packaged foods, and constantly getting too little sleep. He has continually put his online activities above his work responsibilities, choosing to rob his employer to pay the Internet. The more he does this, the more disconnected, unnoticed, and insignificant he feels in the real world. Which makes his time on the Internet that much more imperative.

Trying to find significance and connection in your life isn't wrong. The problem lies not in *what* you are trying to obtain, but *where* you are trying to obtain it. There is only one source for all of those things in your life, and it isn't online. Through your relationship with your heavenly Father, you can feel connected to the most powerful force in the universe. You can have an influence over your own life and those around you through your prayers. You can discover the significance you already have in God's eyes.

> Ultimately, connection, influence, and significance can be found through only one source.

Nobody likes to be lonely. Even the person who spends all night by himself in front of a computer screen is not really alone in his own mind. He's connecting to other people online. And even though he's the only one in the room, he's surrounded by every other person he has communicated with. It is only when he disconnects from the Internet that he really feels cut off from other people.

Yet no person is totally disconnected, whether on or off the Internet. God has established a connection with every person. That connection is a familial one. God is your Creator, and you are his creation. There can be no deeper or more permanent connection. You will always be his creation, whether you acknowledge him or not.

The connection you crave already exists through a relationship with God. If you have never really considered that possibility, I would encourage you to explore this relationship now. Psalm 139 puts it beautifully:

> O Lord, you have searched me and you know me. You know when I sit and when I rise; you perceive my thoughts from afar. You discern my going out and my lying down; you are familiar with all my ways. . . . For you created my inmost being; you knit me together in my mother's womb. . . . My frame was not hidden from you when I was made in the secret place. When I was woven together in the depths of the earth, your eyes saw my unformed body.

Before you were born, God made a connection with you. Seek to discover this connection.

How much more significance do you need in life than being a child of the living God? A child planned for, loved, provided for? God knows your name, the number of hairs on your head. He knows your inmost thoughts and the deepest desires of your heart. No matter what significance you find on the Internet, it will never come close to your value through God.

How to Change

You have the opportunity to change your orientation to life. You can redirect your life away from the Internet and towards true, personal relationships.

Acknowledge Your Reasons

Before you can change your Internet habits, you need to acknowledge and understand the reasons why you consistently return, over and over again, to the same activities.

> Don't operate on autopilot as far as the Internet is concerned.

Don't operate on autopilot as far as the Internet is concerned. If you have reached a stage where you've become dependent upon the Internet, it will be difficult to alter your behavior unless you gain a clear understanding of just what you are attempting to get out of it, what needs you are looking to fill through the Internet.

One solution is to keep a journal. Leave it near you computer, where you can get at it easily. Write down where you go when you get online. Determine why you are going to each destination and what you hope to get out of your activity there. List anyone you hope to communicate with while you are there. Explain why you are looking forward to conversing with that person. Write these things in order to ascertain why the Internet holds the value it does in your life.

Seek God's Perspective

Scripture is full of examples of how much God loves and cares for you. There are even books containing nothing but God's promises to you from the Bible. Visit your local Christian bookstore and ask about obtaining one of these "Promise books" for use as a daily devotional guide.

Establish or revitalize your prayer life. Ask God to have influence over the areas where you feel the most conviction. Don't exclude God from the passions in your life. Include him, and ask him for wisdom in knowing how to further those causes to his glory.

The Next Step

1. On a piece of paper, record the two-way areas of the

Internet that you frequent. Below each, write down your reasons for engaging in that online activity. List how you feel while engaged in each.

2. Consider this question: Has your desire to connect, to influence, and to have significance overshadowed other priorities in your life? If so, what areas of your life are you shortchanging because of your Internet use?

3. If you frequent specific chat rooms or newsgroups, what group identity are you becoming part of? Would you be as likely to join an actual group addressing these issues, or are you only interested in being part of an online group?

4. On a scale from one to ten (1=lowest; 10=highest), rate how important it is to spend time and energy in the following areas: at home with your spouse, at home with your child(ren), at work, at church, with friends, online. Now, using the same scale, rate the amount of time and energy you are giving in each area. Compare your answers. Is there a correlation between how important you feel it is to invest in an area and how much time and energy you devote to it?

CHAPTER TEN

Shaping a New Reality:

Electronic Fantasy Life

Craig cursed as the yellow light turned red. He braked hard, screeching his tires. He added a screech of his own. His boss was going to be ticked.

Not that Craig cared all that much. He hated his job. What he liked were the hours. He worked at the supermarket until midnight. As soon as he got home, he hopped online, still wide awake. That's when his *real* life began.

At work, time clicked on relentlessly as he stocked shelves, broke down cardboard boxes, and packed other people's stuff into brown paper bags. Hours of smiling politely at customers who treated him as if he were no more important than a light fixture. Hours of telling people where the pancake syrup was. All the while thinking back to his time on the computer the night before and looking ahead to when he could log on again.

Craig spent his days being told what to do, where to go, how to act, and what to say. But he could return home to find solace in the role-playing games he enjoyed on the Internet. There, he could don the mantle of a wizard and be all-knowing, all-powerful. Or maybe he'd be an elf. Highly intelligent and puckish, he played with a devil-may-care attitude, blowing off steam and just being crazy.

He'd started with role-playing games years earlier, in the Dark Ages before computers. Dungeons and Dragons had been the first, but by no means the last. In high school, dueling against other players with his wits was more engaging than the brute physicality of sports like baseball or football. It was his imagination that was well-muscled.

Lately, though, the games had begun to feel too limiting and restrictive. So Craig began spending more of his computing time in a variety of Internet chat rooms. There, he could meet others, engage in verbal sparring on a wide range of topics—all while playing a character entirely of his own creation. On the computer, he had complete freedom. He was free to answer whatever questions he wanted, however he wanted, with whatever information he wanted—real or imagined.

More and more, he viewed himself in terms of his online persona. That was the real Craig. "Craig, the supermarket stock clerk" was the fantasy.

The Power of Imagination

Which of us, when we were little, didn't spend hours in a fairy-tale world of childhood fantasy? Which of us, as children, didn't imagine ourselves fighting bravely for truth and justice? Who didn't share secrets with invisible friends or dream we could fly or that we possessed astonishing, magical powers?

In childhood, these diversions into fantasy had a great deal of meaning and value. The fantasy world is all about learning. Learning the joy of stretching your mind beyond what you can see and touch. Learning how to think beyond where you are right now. Learning how you might react in a given situation. Learning simply how to play and create out of nothing but the contents of your own imagination.

For most adults, the lure of the fantasy world becomes tempered with a mature acknowledgment of responsibility and the pressures of everyday life. We come to relish those few hours when we can take a boat out and pretend, if for a moment, that

> **The Internet can be one enormous escape hatch.**

we're commanding a mighty sailing vessel. A few hours spent in a hammock, lost in the latest bestseller, are now sheer heaven. Fantasy for adults is about escaping reality. We live in a stressful world. We face a great deal of competing demands. Much of this stress we create for ourselves by deciding we need to do too many things. And so, to relieve this pressure, we spend our leisure time finding ways to escape.

Sometimes the Internet can be one enormous escape hatch.

Fighting the Urge to Falsify

We all want to better ourselves. It's part of the maturing process. By understanding and confronting our weaknesses and faults, we work toward growing beyond them and becoming better people. In this case, the journey is at least as important as the destination. Invaluable life lessons are learned along the way to personal improvement.

The Internet, however, provides a deceptive shortcut. There, personal improvement can come at the click of a mouse button. There is no journey to take, no struggle, no lesson, only the appearance of arrival. Online, you can claim to be better than you really are and no one will know anything different. You can claim to be honest, forthright, and a person of integrity, all the time lying with complete impunity.

Seasoned Netizens are aware that the level of honesty on the Internet is in constant flux, depending on whom they are communicating with at any given time. Some people, in fact, even feel that the anonymity of the Internet allows them to be *more* honest than they would be in person. And, although we may start out intending simply to be ourselves, our idea about how that really plays out in cyberspace may change without our realizing it.

Habits come upon us, sometimes without our even being aware of them. Have you ever known people who exhibited an unconscious habit of throat clearing, checking their watch, or twirling their hair? Chances are, they are wholly unaware of it. They acquired their habit by doing it over and over without really thinking about it. Habits evolve through repetition. If you repeatedly fabricate details of your life and personality on the Internet, a habit of deception will develop. And if it works in one area of your life, you may be tempted to incorporate it into others.

You wouldn't think of telling someone you're a mathematical genius and a professional model if you're not. But might you shave off a couple of pounds or increase your SAT scores by a hundred points? The anonymity of the Internet can be a draw to exaggerate the truth, falsify essential details, or flat out lie in response to an uncomfortable question. And while the person you are speaking to has no clue you're lying through your teeth, there is someone who does.

God is about truth. God expects us to be truthful to each other (Zech. 8:16; Col. 3:9). There isn't a list of "Exceptions to Truth Telling" included in Scripture. In fact, Jesus considers truth to be so valuable that he calls himself the Truth (John 14:6). Embellishing the truth just isn't an acceptable activity.

A Way of Escape

The real world for you may be so dismal, so bleak, that escaping through the Internet may seem like an acceptable alternative. *At least there,* you think, *I can make my life everything I really want it to be.*

No matter how unpleasant your life is right now, escaping online can't change it. The Internet may numb the pain for you, but it cannot transform your life. Consider this: The time and energy you are using to change your life on the Internet would be better spent confronting and dealing with your life for real.

Any freedom you gain online ceases to exist the minute you log off. The Internet isn't going to give you sustainable freedom. Only acknowledging the truth about your life can do that. Listen to what Jesus wants you to know about hiding and about truth: "You will know the truth, and the truth will set you free" (John 8:32).

It may appear as though your Internet identity is helping you cope with your life, but it only puts off reality for a little while. Life is waiting for you every time you sign off. And sometimes it has gotten worse while you've been gone. Maintaining emotional health in the midst of a difficult situation is going to require all of your strength and stamina. It will require you to be alert and aware of how real events are affecting you. And it will require seeking out real help to change your circumstances instead of changing the truth to escape the circumstances.

> Fantasy is alluring because it never has to deal with the nuts and bolts of reality.

Fantasy is alluring because it never has to deal with the nuts and bolts of reality. Fantasy can sanitize any situation, bleaching out the problems and frustrations, leaving a pure-white canvas on which to paint an impossible portrait of life. Reality doesn't have that option. It can't duck paying the bills, dealing with the boss, coping with an angry spouse, battling the flu, or confronting a disobedient child.

This draw of fantasy seems to especially affect people who fantasize about who they are on the Internet through chat rooms and e-mail. Someone who is married, who lives a fantasy life on the Internet as a single person without family obligations, may become so enamored with the perceived freedom of the imagined life that he or she leaves spouse and family. Even if the fantasy is never played out in reality, the false security of the fantasy may sour your perception of reality.

Two Worlds

There are two worlds in which we actually interact with others: the physical world around us and the spiritual world around God. When it comes to true one-on-one relationships, there is no room for fantasy.

This is not meant as an indictment of imagination. Without imagination, we could not set goals for the future, plan ahead, or create a vision of something we'd like to build. Without imagination, it would be impossible to grasp the concept of deity, something completely outside of ourselves. Through your imagination, you are able to read Scripture and visualize such things as angels, demons, faith, and heaven. Obsessive use of that same imagination to hide from yourself, shirk your responsibilities, or willfully lie to other people on the Internet is a gross misuse of this gift.

Unlimited fantasy excursions are hardly different from numbing yourself through drugs or alcohol or any number of destructive behaviors. Fantasy has no power to bring you closer to the truth, which will set you free. If you desire a connection with other people, to have an intimacy about your relationships, seek out God and other people in the real world.

How to Change

If you are spending hours online taking on a different persona, stop and take a look at the nature of the character or characters you are hiding behind. What is it about those characters that appeals to you? Do you wish you could be more like them in your real life? Have you ever tried to respond to a real-life situation as your online persona would?

Determine today to conduct your relationships online in truth. Discontinue any that are based solely on falsehood—those in which you have fabricated details of your life. The anonymity you have hidden behind should make it easier for you to sever such relationships completely. However, be honest about the reason why you are severing the relationship. Your honesty may encourage others to consider doing likewise.

> Determine today to conduct your relationships online in truth.

There are aspects of your life that should be off-limits to others, especially if you are married. Avoid them. Clearly explain your boundaries and hold others accountable to respecting those boundaries.

Use your relationships for the betterment of yourself and for the betterment of those you communicate with. Be transparent and honest, while maintaining the proper boundaries for those communications. Allow the light of Christ to shine through your communications instead of obscuring the truth through dishonesty and fantasy.

The Next Step

1. Write down the three characteristics you wish you possessed in real life and are bestowing on your online personas. Outline a plan for incorporating more of each into your real life. For example, if you have given your persona great physical strength, consider joining a health club or taking up jogging or swimming to strengthen your body. You'll improve your health, and you'll be partici-

pating in a beneficial activity that has nothing to do with the Internet.

2. Think back over your recent Internet use. Have you been using your online activities to escape a particular situation at home? at work? with a particular person? Has this situation gotten better or worse while you've been online? Investigate ways of facing up to the issues and working through them.

3. What are some other ways you avoid dealing with unpleasant situations? Do you smoke, binge eat, drink alcohol, or take drugs? Have you ever combined one of those responses with your Internet use? Do you combine any of them regularly?

4. Ask God to help you to desire to live in the real world with other people and to relate to him in spirit and in truth. Ask for the Holy Spirit's help to recognize the lies in your life that have become like the truth to you.

CHAPTER ELEVEN

Viewing Online Pornography:

Visiting the Back Alleys from Home

Daryl couldn't believe it had gone this far. He kept looking at the Visa bill, hoping futilely that he had somehow misread the thing. But each time he went over the figures, they added up the same. It hadn't seemed like so much at the time, but at $39.95 for fifteen minutes of online viewing, it just kept adding up. The money limit he'd set for the entire month got bypassed within a week.

Vicky was going to kill him. She'd look at him with those big, hurt eyes and ask the one question he adamantly did not want to answer. The whole thing would open up an ugly Pandora's box of stuff he'd rather keep locked up tight. What was he going to do? There had to be a way to answer her question without giving away, or giving up, too much.

It was his work's fault. All that stress. His online time was a reward for a job well done, an earned bonus at the end of a hectic week.

Then there was the fact that Vicky and little Daryl had gone away to visit her family for almost two full weeks. What was he supposed to do with her gone? Things between them had been less than solid over the past seven or eight months anyway, and he had needs. If she couldn't see her way clear to do her duty as his wife, how could she fault him for finding a creative way to take care of his needs? It's not as though he was out cruising the streets. He wasn't having an affair. And he wasn't hanging out in some storefront with paper-covered windows or at a truck stop along the interstate. This was in the privacy of his own home.

Nobody was getting hurt. In fact, it was nothing more than a business transaction. After all, he was an adult. Wasn't he allowed to buy whatever he wanted? He was merely a consumer paying for a service. Obviously, those who provided the service didn't have a problem with what he was doing. That was their business—and, frankly, this was his.

But, now. Well, the only way to pay the current bill was to take some of their money out of savings. Vicky didn't keep track of the day-to-day stuff, but she did care about their savings account. It was her airline ticket home to her parents . . . the refrigerator she knew they'd have to replace soon . . . the money for Daryl's private preschool. There was no way she'd overlook this much money vanishing from their account.

He could always lie some more and tell her it was for something else. But thinking about the spiral he'd been in for over half a year, he realized he didn't want it to continue. The whole thing had gotten out of hand.

The simple truth was, there was no way to explain it all away. He would just have to come clean, tell Vicky, and hope for the best. Good thing little Daryl was too young to understand what all the shouting would be about.

The New Red Light District

What is pornography? The short answer is that pornography is explicit, sexual imagery—whether visual, auditory, written, or a combination—that creates a state of sexual excitement.

For decades the legal community has struggled to come up with a legal definition of pornography that separates pornography from legitimate artistic expression. But the legal standard has allowed for a wide variety of pornographic material due to its narrow definition of obscenity. Obscene material is generally defined as sexually explicit material having no redeeming value. Because of this narrow definition of obscenity, and because of the difficulty in regulating the Internet,

> Because of the difficulty in regulating the Internet, much pornography is available online.

much pornography is available online. Some of it is pornography involving children, and some pedophiles (those who sexually abuse children) use the Internet to seek young victims.

God created sex when he created males and females. God does not create sinful activity. Instead, it is we who pervert God's purposes and bring about sin. God instituted marriage from the beginning of the world and created a relationship within which his gift of sexual intercourse could bless people. Of course, there are many married couples who strive to live out God's intentions for human sexuality. But there are also others who move sex and sexual activity out of the bounds of marriage and into sinful areas. One of these sinful areas is pornography.

God is not vague about pornography. Pornography directly and adversely affects the sacred relationship of husband and wife—as well as other male-female relationships.

Sexual union is a sacred act, designed by God to be exclusive to marriage. Genesis does not record any physical union between Adam and Eve (Gen. 4:1) until after God refers to them as husband and wife (Gen. 2:24; 3:6). It is the sexual union within marriage that causes the two distinct individuals to become one flesh. When husbands and wives become one flesh, their bodies unite physically, emotionally, and spiritually. They are no longer exclusively their own but belong to each other (1 Cor. 7:2-4). Any sexual activity that occurs between a person and someone other than a spouse is called adultery.

Societal standards regarding sex outside of marriage, marriage itself, and adultery have changed over the past several decades. What used to be considered socially wrong and even illegal is now accepted without comment. There is little societal stigma attached to sexual activity outside of marriage. Now those issues are considered a private matter, just between the parties involved.

Wait a minute, you may be thinking. *I'm not committing adultery. And I'm not sleeping with someone I'm not married to. All I'm doing is looking at pictures, tiny dots on a computer screen. What is so wrong with that?* Consider Jesus' words in Matthew 5:27-28: "You have heard that it was said, 'Do not commit adultery.' But I tell you that anyone who looks at a woman lustfully has already committed adultery with her in his heart." And that is the very goal of pornography, to stir up the emotions and elicit a sexual response that will keep you coming back for more.

To satisfy the yearnings that pornography instills, the majority of viewers rely on masturbation. But the effects of this activity do not end with a climax. Using pornography as an impetus for sexual arousal can, over time, affect the way we perceive and interact with the opposite sex in the course of our daily lives. In addition, while masturbation may temporarily curb sexual desires, it only fuels the desire to masturbate again when feeling sexually aroused. It can become a consuming habit.

If you are married, you made a vow to look to your spouse exclusively as the source of your sexual fulfillment. You vowed to use sexual arousal and its fulfillment as a bond of intimacy in your union. By engaging in sexual activity apart from your spouse, that bond is broken and the relationship suffers. Your very human and flawed spouse must contend with a physically perfect, air-brushed image on a screen. And because the entire personality of that pictured creature springs straight from your

> You might find yourself relying more and more on the Web and less and less on your spouse.

own mind—existing solely to meet your needs in exactly the way you desire—your spouse will never be able to compete. Real-life sex could seem pretty mundane after all of that. You might find yourself relying more and more on the Web and less and less on your spouse.

The Power to Harm

First Corinthians 6:18 tells all of us—married and single—to flee from sexual immorality. But it is hard to flee sexual immorality if you've made a conscious decision to hop online and visit a pornographic site or newsgroup. Viewing pornography on the Internet will not bring you closer to God or help you to deal constructively with your natural sexual desires. Rather, pornography in general, and on the Internet specifically, has the power to damage and destroy relationships.

In California, a veterinarian lost his license because of his addiction to online pornography. He spent so much time at work looking at pornography, he trained an unschooled assistant to conduct exams and surgeries so his viewing wouldn't be disturbed. This assistant took over the business of running his veterinary practice. Of course, that wasn't something that could go unnoticed forever. His clients noticed. His colleagues noticed. So did the State of California. It cost him his professional license and his livelihood.

Because he spent so much time at home looking at pornography, his wife refused to put up with it any longer and left. It cost him his marriage.

Because of the nature of the pornography he viewed, it was deemed inappropriate for him to have unsupervised contact with minors. It cost him his children.

Because of the depth of his interest in pornography, people were curious and his obsession became public knowledge. It cost him his dignity.

Pornography has a cost and users pay it.

Do not underestimate the power of online pornographic images. They have the power over time to bind sexual excitement to themselves. If the images are violent or homosexual in nature—and you reinforce those images with your own sexual arousal—you may set up a pattern where only those images can produce a sexual response in you. In other words, merely having sex may no longer be enough.

Pornography drives a wedge in your relationships with your spouse and others. It colors how you view all members of the opposite sex.

There is also the cost to those people involved in its manufacture. God calls his people to be the body of Christ on this earth. Christ gave up his rights and position to serve people, even to the point of death on a cross. Our desires and needs do not give us the right to exploit other people. The next time you decide to view pornography on the Internet, visualize that woman not as a mere object for your sexual excitement but as someone's daughter, mother, or sister. Think of her as someone for whom Christ has died. (We speak primarily of female images, as the vast majority of pornography users are men.)

> Pornography colors how you view all members of the opposite sex.

Guilt and remorse should be a by-product of your online pornography. If you don't think you feel guilty, ask yourself this question: When was the last time you included it in a letter to your folks? Or brought it up while conversing with your twelve-year-old daughter at the breakfast table? Or broached the subject while talking to your minister after church services? Or informed your wife you were going to go online for a little pornography before you joined her in bed?

Learning to Take Control

Maybe you got hooked on Internet pornography without meaning to. You weren't really looking for pornography in the first place. You just hopped onto the Net and typed in something that took you to a place you didn't want to go . . . at first. You never meant for it to go as far or as long as it has.

It is the classic scenario of the chocolate eclair in the refrigerator. You go past a bakery on your way home. You weren't planning to buy an eclair, but, all of a sudden, there it is. It looks really good, so you go in and buy it. You stare at the eclair on the seat beside you on the drive home. You know you really shouldn't eat the eclair. It's not good for you; it's loaded with calories and fat. You convince yourself you shouldn't have bought it in the first place, and you're not going to eat it. When you get home, you put it in the fridge and say to yourself, "I have the willpower to say no to that eclair." Eventually, everyone else in the house goes to bed. You're watching the news, a little hungry. After all, it's been almost four-and-a-half hours since dinner. But in the back of your mind, you know there's a chocolate eclair in the fridge. You told yourself you wouldn't eat it. In fact, for most of the evening you didn't even think about it. But now you're hungry and no one else is up, and you know it's in there. What do you do? Are you sure you won't give in and eat the eclair?

Of course, viewing pornography is not really like eating an eclair. But the solution to one has application to the other. What is the one way to be sure you won't eat the eclair? Don't buy it in the first place. But maybe you've already bought it. If you really had no plans to eat the eclair, you would have immediately thrown it out when you arrived home. You might have said you weren't going to eat the eclair, but by putting it in the fridge, your actions indicated you intended doing just the opposite.

Ask yourself if you're one of those who put eclairs in the fridge when it comes to pornography. Your words to yourself—and perhaps to others—indicate you have every intention of controlling yourself in regard to the Internet and pornography, but your actions indicate the opposite. You may say you can control yourself, but your actions are saying it's the timing you're able to control. You are able to put off the when, but not the whether. When you feel it's safe, then you take the eclair out of the fridge, carefully, with anticipation.

There's only one thing to do to show that you are really in control. When it comes to your use of pornography on the Internet, it's time to throw out the eclair. You need to get the pornography out of your life, even if it means getting rid of your computer. It simply isn't worth destroying the most important relationships in life.

How to Clothe Yourself

Colossians 3:5 is quite specific about how we are to respond to immorality: "Put to death, therefore, whatever belongs to your earthly nature: sexual immorality, impurity, lust, evil desires and greed, which is idolatry." We are to get rid of those things. But that is just the first step in a two-step process. The next step is to fill our lives with something better. Verse 12 says, "Therefore, as God's chosen people, holy and dearly loved, clothe yourselves with compassion, kindness, humility, gentleness and patience." Verse 17 caps the chapter by saying, "And whatever you do, whether in word or deed, do it all in the name of the Lord Jesus, giving thanks to God the Father through him."

Philippians 4:8 puts it this way: "Finally, brothers, whatever is true, whatever is noble, whatever is right, whatever is pure, whatever is lovely, whatever is admirable—if anything is excellent or praiseworthy—think about such things." If what you do, if what you view, on the Internet is not true, noble, right, pure, lovely, or admirable, stop doing it and stop viewing it.

How to Change

Make the commitment now to stop. Does it mean you have to give up the Internet completely? That depends on you.

Taking Steps to Stop

Try the following suggestions:

- Move the computer into a common area of the house, in full view of other family members. Allow scrutiny to act as an inhibitor.

- Don't use the computer when no one else is there. Consider putting a lock on the hard drive and giving your wife the key. If you can't use it, you can't abuse it.

- Put systems in place that will provide a buffer against your impulses when you are weak. Subscribe to an online service that restricts access to pornographic sites, even if it means changing the online company you're with now.

- Put a picture of Jesus near the computer or set up an empty chair near you while you're online to remind yourself you're really not alone.

- If you are unable to control using the Internet without being drawn to pornography, don't use it. Go back to making phone calls and writing letters. Go back to using the Yellow Pages and the local library.

Whatever you do, get help. Don't make this your secret or your family's secret. Find capable, trustworthy counsel and seek advice.

Take time to seriously think about the hows and the whys of your Internet pornography compulsion. Use this as an opportunity to better yourself, to turn an error into an opportunity to take stock, and to improve your character. God will bless your efforts.

The Next Step

1. Write down a confession of your online pornographic use. Include the reasons you are viewing pornography and what you feel when you do. Write down the excuses you have always said to yourself to justify viewing pornography.
2. Which Scripture verses were the most meaningful to bring to light the error of those excuses?
3. If you are married, go to your spouse, explain your situation, and ask for forgiveness. Work together to find healing and a solution to your problem.
4. Spend time in prayer with God, asking for forgiveness and wisdom about how to bring your desires under control.
5. Get a software package that filters out pornographic sites. Check *Consumer Reports* or another testing service to see which ones work best. (Some are nearly useless.)
6. In thirty days, if you have not made progress to significantly decrease your use of pornography, seek professional help from a counselor specializing in addictions or compulsive disorders.

CHAPTER TWELVE

Responsibilities and Relationships:

Does Connecting Mean Disconnecting?

There was nothing Greg liked better than hopping online. He found himself in front of the keyboard almost every evening and on the weekends. His computer at work had Internet access, too, and Greg often surfed the Net on his lunch hour. Well, he had to admit, sometimes that hour stretched itself out a little if he found something really interesting. At home, he kept up with his e-mail, checked his personal finances by tracking stocks and mutual funds, and participated in a few chat rooms. He never meant to spend as much time as he did online, but it was all so fascinating that the time just flew by.

Of course, his wife wasn't thrilled. She complained she never got to spend any time with him.

His kids had stopped asking if he'd help them with their homework or play a game. He had offered to do something with them on the computer, but they often wanted to do things outside. Greg figured he had come up with so many excuses that they just didn't bother to ask anymore.

His coworkers had lately started giving him a bad time about Net surfing when he was supposed to be working.

He used to belong to a fraternal organization, but he stopped going to the meetings because he just couldn't find the time every third Thursday.

On Sunday mornings, Fran usually took the kids by herself to church because Saturday night was prime Net time, and he just couldn't make that early service anymore.

While Greg was busy connecting to life online, he didn't realize he was disconnecting from all of the other relationships in his life.

Maintaining a Balance

With competing demands on your time and energy, how do you maintain a balance in life? If going online allows you to put the cares of the day behind you, for just a little while, how can you balance that with the fact that you have a spouse who wants to talk to you, kids who need your attention, or friends who deserve some quality time?

> With competing demands on your time and energy, how do you maintain a balance in life?

Your unhealthy relationship to the Internet can damage the other relationships in your life. The cost is real and must be paid—usually by those close to you.

Relationships on the Job

Just as colleges are finding that student access to the Internet is having unanticipated negative side effects, workplaces are also finding their employees' online activities do not always add up to a bonus for the business. Many businesses are limiting employees to strictly work-related Internet searches and restricting personal e-mail messages. Employers do not want to subsidize their employees' personal Internet activities.

Businesses are not just affected by on-site Internet activity. When an employee spends too much time on the Internet at home, it can affect his or her ability to perform on the job the following day.

God expects you to carry out your responsibilities in a mature way that speaks well of him and your relationship with him. The people at work are watching to see how you act and whether your faith in God is something that is real and heartfelt. One of the most important barometers they have is how well you do your job. Don't let your Internet use dilute your witness to your working world.

Relationships at Home
If you are caring for children, you have an obligation to give them what they need to grow into healthy, mature adults. One of the things children need most is your time. It is not just the quality of time that is important, it is also the quantity of time. Your children need you to be around them, carrying on day-to-day life so they can watch you and learn from you. They need to work with you, have fun with you, relax with you. It would be a tragedy if all your children learned from you was what other things in your life you considered more valuable. When you consistently choose to interact with the Internet instead of your children, you are sending a clear signal of where they stand in your priorities.

Responsible in Marriage
Your spouse isn't necessarily being selfish by wanting you to get off the computer. He or she just wants more time with you. You can determine how much time you're willing to give, but you cannot determine how much time he or she *needs*. Have you tracked how much time you spend online? Add to that how

much time you think about being online. And how much time you spend reading and talking about computers and online stuff.

Then figure out how much free time you have—time when you're not working, sleeping, or eating. Calculate the percentage of time you're devoting to the computer—actual online time and time spent thinking or talking about it. Compare that with how much time you spend interacting with your spouse. (*Interacting* means doing things together, engaging in joint activities, not just being in the same place at the same time. In other words, interacting doesn't mean you are in the chair with the laptop and a modem connection while your spouse is watching television.) How does your time interacting with your spouse compare with the amount of time you're giving to being online?

What reasons are you giving yourself for how much time you spend online? What reasons are you giving your spouse? What would you do if your spouse spent the same amount of time that you're spending online with, say, another person? Would you begin to view that person as a competitor? (The correct answer is not, "I wouldn't care. I'd just spend more time on the computer"!)

In marriage, there is the reasonable expectation that you will not allow any other activity to damage or detract from your relationship with your spouse. When you insist upon spending so much time on the Internet, thus neglecting time with your spouse, you are breaking one of the fundamental covenants of life.

Responsible for Your Spiritual Relationship

God knew you in your mother's womb (Ps. 139:13). He knew you as your days were beginning and knows how many days you have left (Ps.139:15-16). He already has a relationship with you—as Creator to created, Father to child, Savior to lost. If you have a relationship to Jesus Christ as Savior, you have an obligation to explore that relationship. Like any relationship, this requires you to spend time together. God would certainly like to hold as important a position in your life as that faceless person you've been sending e-mail to for the last three months. If you've got time to compose those messages, you have time to spend in prayer.

Avoiding Dangerous Relationships
Communication on the Internet can quickly take on a personal, intimate tone, given the environment of anonymity in which it occurs. If you are meeting regularly with someone else online and discussing personal and private matters, especially of an intimate nature, you may be headed for trouble, particularly if you are married. The individual you are

> There is mounting evidence of people leaving established relationships to seek out those they've met online.

pouring out your heart to may truly be a stranger to you. Everything he or she told you could be sheer fabrication. You may be risking your marriage, your emotions, your money—all for a lie.

Yet people do it. There is mounting evidence of people leaving their established relationships to begin new, real-life relationships with those they've met online. People have left spouses, cities, even countries to physically connect with those to whom they have already connected electronically. The allure of the online relationship causes the other relationships in life to pale by comparison.

The danger to relationships can be twofold, encompassing both the amount of time spent online and the kinds of connections made while online.

Responsible Relationships

Should you totally avoid any sort of relationship online? Of course not. Everyone has more than one relationship in life, and most people are able to handle their various relationships without causing damage. Family members, coworkers, casual acquaintances, good friends—these relationships can and should bring dimension and satisfaction to your life. No one person is going to be able to fill all of your needs. But you need to realize that your acceptance of those relationships obligates you to maintain them and handle competing relationships responsibly.

The key to handling online relationships is basic common sense. In any relationship, there are certain cautions to keep in mind to help define the limits of propriety. Adults should not enter into intimate situations with children. Married people should not enter into intimate relationships with someone other than their spouse. Single people should avoid situations where their values and morals are likely to be compromised.

Internet relationships are no different.

Keep Your Eyes Open
With text-only communications, there are no physical clues to help you determine the veracity of what you are being told. What you see (or read) is not necessarily what you're really going to get. Keep that in mind every time you enter into a discussion on the Internet with someone you don't know. Be careful not to take blindly as fact everything he or she tells you.

Don't Set Yourself Up for Problems
The anonymous nature of online correspondence tends to fast-forward communications toward the intimate. Be prepared. Like glancing in someone's window without meaning to, reading intimate messages may cause you to take a second look. If you do nothing to indicate that this is an area of discussion you will not engage in, it will be taken as approval to continue or even delve deeper. Avoid chat rooms or bulletin boards devoted to intimate or sexual content. Once you're headed down the

wrong road, it's a lot harder to get back than if you had never started at all.

Set Limits on What You Share
Personal information is compelling. If it weren't, daytime television would be vastly different than it is today. Limit the amount of personal information you both elicit from someone online and give to someone upon request.

Don't Answer If You Don't Want To
No matter how compelling a request for information is, you are still totally in control of what information you give out. Just because you've been asked something doesn't mean you have to reply. If a question steps into an area you know you should avoid, politely but firmly express your intention not to answer or to continue the conversation along that vein. If the person you're conversing with attempts to cajole, tease, manipulate, or simply pester you about it, it's time to sever that relationship.

No matter how compelling an online relationship is, if it becomes inappropriate, you need to take steps to fix it. You have the power to alter an online relationship, redefine it, or end it.

Taking Control

Using the computer wisely involves controlling your impulses and behavior. With the speed of the computer, the breadth of the Web, and the diversity of the Internet, the consequences of not controlling your impulses are magnified. You can get into more trouble, more quickly, with more negative effects than with anything else you've experienced before.

You can lose track of time and responsibilities by visiting just one more site, sending one more message, reading one more discussion. You can trade the sensory experience of the outdoors for the insular, controlled space of four walls. You can lose touch with real life and get immersed in a self-designed world. You can forego the immediate and intimate presence of real people for the seductive and deceptive realm of online relationships. You can supplant the beauty of married sexuality for the one-sided, instant gratification of pornography.

Shouldn't your time be used to better advantage? After an evening of surfing the Net or posting on a bulletin board, how much have you really accomplished? How much has that activity added to your life, made you a better person, endeared you to your family and friends? Shouldn't your family be more important to you than what you do online? They are the real people who surround you and love you. They care about you and only want to be able to spend more time with you.

If you honestly cannot control your Internet use, it is time to accept your limitations and go offline. At this point in your life, you're just not capable of handling the temptations the Internet represents for you. While this may seem severe, there are some things that just aren't worth the risk. In Matthew 5:29-30, Jesus makes a rather gruesome statement:

> If your right eye causes you to sin, gouge it out and throw it away. It is better for you to lose one part of your body than for your whole body to be thrown into hell. And if your right hand causes you to sin, cut it off and throw it away. It is better for you to lose one part of your body than for your whole body to go into hell.

This is not a proof text for self-mutilation. Jesus uses hyperbole to make a very important point about the process of sin. Sin begins with temptation. Sin begins with the evil desires of the heart in response to temptation. If the eye is tempted by seeing something that contributes to the heart's evil desires, it needs to be gouged out. If the hand is tempted to do something that contributes to the heart's evil desires, it needs to be cut off. No part of the body is worth losing your eternal soul over. This is the really long view.

How to Change

If you are not convinced of the Internet's influence over you and your activities, take a self-imposed break from online activity. Restrain from Internet activities for a specific amount of time—a month, say. Choose a time when you normally would have access to the Internet. In other words, the month you decide to forego online time should not be the same month your family takes a cross-country trip to visit relatives. To assess the extent of your online reliance, you need to be able to say no within the context of your normal Internet use.

> Learn how to use the Internet responsibly and avoid situations that compound your compulsion to abuse it.

Of course, stopping computer use completely may not be an option. Some business people, journalists, researchers, educators, and consultants, for example, cannot simply turn off their Internet access. They face the very same problem that people with eating disorders face. They may no more be able to stop using the Internet than a bulimic can stop eating. If you are one of these people for whom the Internet is a required part of your work and life, the only option you have is to learn how to use the Internet responsibly and avoid situations that tend to compound your compulsion to abuse it. If you find this to be beyond your ability, consider either choosing a different way to do your job, or finding a different job. Look for a job that will not require you to spend time on the Internet until you can control your use of it.

As you have determined where your problem areas with the

Internet lie, believe in your ability to control your use. If you don't think you can control yourself, you won't. Resolve to seek the help you need to take back control over your life and your activities. Find out the reasons why you feel you cannot live without doing what you're doing online. Find out where that feeling is coming from and tackle it, head-on, with the help of a counselor, therapist, clergy member, or friend.

For most people, the Internet need not be an all-or-nothing activity. The proper precautions can help guard you from its dangers. Taking precautions is not only for someone who has a serious problem. After all, you don't use a jackhammer without ear plugs and goggles. You don't go inline skating without wearing protective padding and a helmet. These activities have the potential to cause damage. That doesn't mean you don't do them; it means you do them wisely.

Establish a schedule for yourself. Decide how much time is appropriate for you to spend on the computer, given your other commitments and responsibilities. Discuss your decision with those people whom your computer use directly affects, including friends and family. Then stick to the schedule.

If time ceases to have any meaning once you get online, get yourself a small, digital timer. (Ticking kitchen timers will probably drive you, and everyone around you, crazy.) When the timer goes off, shut down the computer.

Whatever you do, don't rely on another person to act as your own personal Cyber Cop. It has the potential to seriously strain your relationship as he or she attempts to do what you've asked ("Help me stick to my schedule!"), while you keep changing the rules ("Just a few minutes more?"). You are the one who must learn to say no.

Making the Right Choices

All of life is about making choices. Where to live, what to

do, whom to be with. Whether or not to use a computer and go online is just another choice in the myriad of options you face.

With all of the resources available to help you make a wise choice, don't forget your best resource. God is the source of wisdom and knowledge. Only he can help you determine if you should be online, and he can also guide you as you integrate the computer into your daily life.

> The computer is a tool that can take you to places you couldn't dream of.

There is nothing inherently good or evil about the computer. If used properly, the computer is a tool that can take you to places you couldn't dream of, accomplish important business, and introduce you to interesting people. It is a gateway, and you determine where you go.

The computer is also a mirror. Our decisions about where we go on it and what we do with it reflect who we are. If you've seen a side of yourself you're not pleased with shining back at you from that monitor, choose to do better. Choose to reflect the person Jesus calls you to be.

Change is possible. It happens all the time. It is called renewal. Let this passage encourage you to strive to do better, to regain control:

> And so, dear brothers and sisters, I plead with you to give your bodies to God. Let them be a living and holy sacrifice—the kind he will accept. When you think of what he has done for you, is this too much to ask? Don't copy the behavior and customs of this world, but let God transform you into a new person by changing the way you think. Then you will know what God wants you to do, and you will know how good and pleasing and perfect his will really is. (Romans 12:1-2, NLT)

You will also be able to know God's will for you regarding the Internet.

The Next Step

1. Make a list of all your relationships, according to the priority you give them. On a separate list, calculate the amount of time you spend on each relationship, from where you spend the most amount of time down to where you spend the least. Compare the two lists.

2. Determine the top family relationship you have and commit to spending an extra hour this week devoted solely to that relationship.

3. Write down any online relationships you have. Estimate the amount of time each week you spend devoted to those relationships. Indicate whether or not you know the person only through the Internet.

   As you look at your relationships, both online and offline, write down what needs of yours each relationship fills. Be prepared to share with a loved one how much you value the relationship with him or her.

4. Spend time in prayer giving each relationship you have listed to God. Ask him to reveal to you any relationships that violate his will. Ask for forgiveness and for the strength to make the necessary changes.

A Final Word

The Internet isn't going to disappear tomorrow. If anything, statistics show that computers will permeate even further into society, and the Internet will continue to gain users at an exponential rate. Cyberspace is only going to grow in size and influence. That's reality.

There are three basic responses to this reality. One response is to vow vehemently not to have anything to do with the Internet. The second is to plunge headlong into cyberspace, heedless of any warnings about its dangers. The third response is to approach it with caution and discretion.

Boycotting Cyberspace

You may have decided the Internet is simply not worth the risks involved. You have a right to decide not to use it.

But if you decide not to use the Internet, choose to do so with a positive attitude. Be prepared for more and more looks of astonishment when people find out you're not online. Anticipate being considered quaintly anachronistic. Be ready to reasonably explain why you choose to use other forms of communication and education. Your explanation can provide an opportunity for you to witness about your values and faith, how you filter your choices in life through your understanding of God.

Avoid any appearance, however, of being "holier than thou." The Internet is used by a great many good people who function well within cyberspace and even contribute to the spreading of God's Word through that medium. The Internet is not evil nor is everyone online engaging in sin. It is a neutral technology whose evil or good is determined by its use.

Refusing to Slow Down

The second response to the reality of Internet influence is to rush on, full-steam ahead, without taking into account the warning signs and responding appropriately. If you have gleaned anything from reading this book, it should be that there are legitimate dangers to be found both on the Internet itself and in its uncontrolled use.

Then again, you may still be refusing to admit you have a problem with the Internet. Admitting that you need to be wise and limit your online activities is not admitting a failure of some kind. On the contrary, it is exhibiting the control necessary to maintain balance in your life. It is not a weakness, it is a strength.

Do not be lulled into thinking that you can disregard Internet warnings because you could never fall prey to its dangers. None of us is immune. We must all be alert to temptation and wise about how to escape.

Use Caution and Discretion

As with any tool capable of being both useful and dangerous, we should approach the Internet with caution and discretion. Consider the following safety tips:

- Avoid the areas that pose a danger to you, whether they are a danger to everyone or whether it is an area in which you are especially vulnerable.
- Constantly evaluate your online activities.
- Keep informed about the latest information regarding Internet trends and use.
- Talk to others who use the Internet and find out how they handle being online.
- If you develop a problem with the Internet, get help immediately.

One God and Father of All

God is a truly amazing Father. He knows you completely. He even knows how you feel about the Internet. He knows whether you hate it or love it. He knows what you do on it and whether your activities are bringing you closer to him or moving you farther away. If you become confused about how to approach the Internet or something on it, pray about it. Ask for God's perspective and wisdom. Stay close and listen to him.

Additional Resources

The following resources are offered as suggestions only and should be approached as you eat fish: You may have to pick out a few bones to get to the meat.

Books

Baker, Jason D. *Christian Cyberspace Companion: A Guide to the Internet and Christian Online Resources* (Baker).

Groothuis, Douglas. *The Soul in Cyberspace* (Baker). Groothuis is a professor at Denver Seminary and writes from a Christian perspective on a variety of subjects relating to spirituality and the Internet.

Horn, Stacy. *Cyberville: Clicks, Culture, and the Creation of an Online Town* (Warner). This book is the story of how Horn created a cyber-community called Echo. It is frank and includes her opinions on a variety of topics relating to the Internet. If you're interested in the type of person who would spend the time and energy devoted to a cyberworld, this is a good jumping-off place.

Hughes, Donna Rice. *Kids Online* (Revell). A book for Christians on the dangers kids face online.

Schultze, Dr. Quentin. *Internet for Christians: Everything You Need to Start Cruising the Net Today* (Partners).

Sherman, Aliza. *Cybergrrl: A Woman's Guide to the World Wide Web* (Ballantine). A guide to specific sites of interest to women and girls. The title comes from Sherman's online name. It includes information on basic topics relating to the Internet.

Young, Dr. Kimberly. *Caught in the Net* (Wiley). This is the book utilizing Young's research on Internet abuse.

Additional Research Papers

Brenner, Victor. "Parameters of Internet Use, Abuse, and Addiction: The first 90 days of the Internet Usage Survey." *Psychological Reports,* 1997. 80:879-882.

Morahan-Martin, Janet and Schumaker, Phyllis. "Incidence and Correlates of Pathological Internet Use." Paper presented at the Annual Convention of the American Psychological Association, August 1997.

Scherer, Kathleen. "College Life Online: Healthy and unhealthy Internet use." Paper presented at the Annual Convention of the American Psychological Association, August 1997.

Resources on Children and Internet Pornography

Aftab, Parry. *A Parents' Guide to the Internet . . . and How to Protect Your Child in Cyberspace* (SC Press).

Berosetin, Deborah. "The Crimebusters Who Save Kids," *Ladies Home Journal* (November 1997).

Britton, Zachary. *Safety Net* (Harvest House). Britton, creator of the Kidshield.com Web site, explores online dangers facing children and provides solutions to keep children safe as they explore the Internet. Written from a Christian perspective.

Isaac, Steven. "Safe Cruising on the Info Highway," *Focus on the Family Magazine* (February 1998). Isaac is associate editor of Focus on the Family's *Plugged In,* which provides reviews and commentary on the latest music, movies, and TV shows.

"Parental Controls," *Smart Computing* (April 1998). This is an excellent article outlining ten of the top parental control software programs currently on the market. It includes information and analysis for each. The magazine has a reputation for being written in plain English.

Web Sites

"Mouse and Potatoes on the Internet: Is the Internet Addictive?" an essay with references can be found at http://members.tripod.com/online/addict.html.

"True Confessions of Life After Internet Addiction," a brief essay, can be found at http://www.chaos.com/netteach/Confess.html.

Other Resources

If you are concerned about the ease of access to pornography on the Internet, you might want to consider a filtered Internet Service Provider that will restrict certain types of information from being accessed through their service. In order to find a list of who these ISPs are and the sort of services they filter and provide, go to a search engine and search for *filtered Internet service providers*. Be prepared to go through a lot of information, because there are many out there. Many are regional ISPs only, so you'll have to check out what's available in your area.

Generally confused about computers and the Internet? Try one of the ... *for Dummies* books written for people who are basically clueless about a computer subject but who are bright and willing to learn. They are available at most large computer stores and bookstores.

The Center

When you're on the Web, visit my home page at www.aplaceof hope.com. There you'll find information on The Center for Counseling and Health Resources, Inc., and information on my seminars and publications. Have a question? Leave it in the comment box.

If you want to hear more about the seminars available, call our toll free seminar information line at 1-888-771-5166 or write me at drgregg@aplaceofhope.net